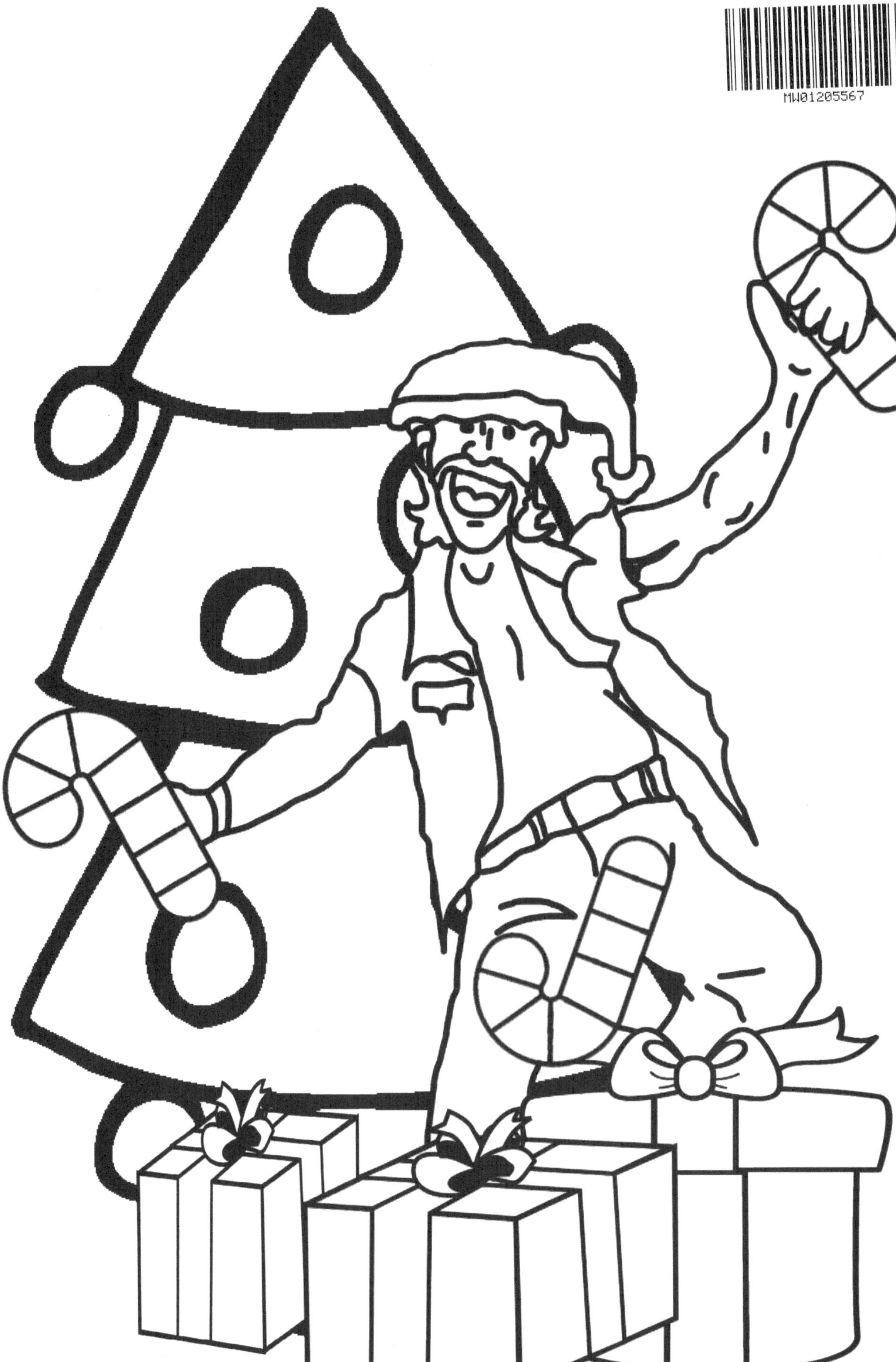

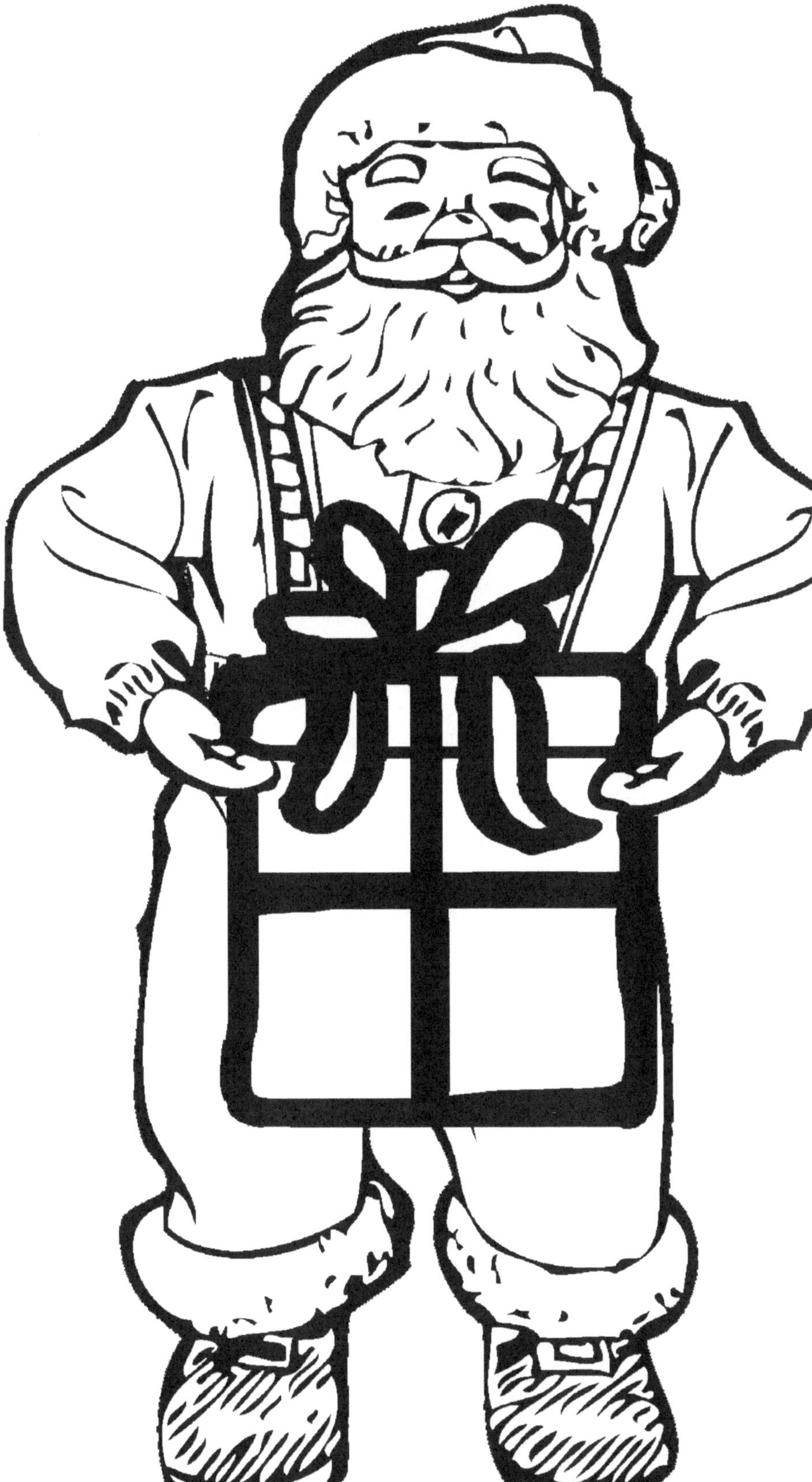

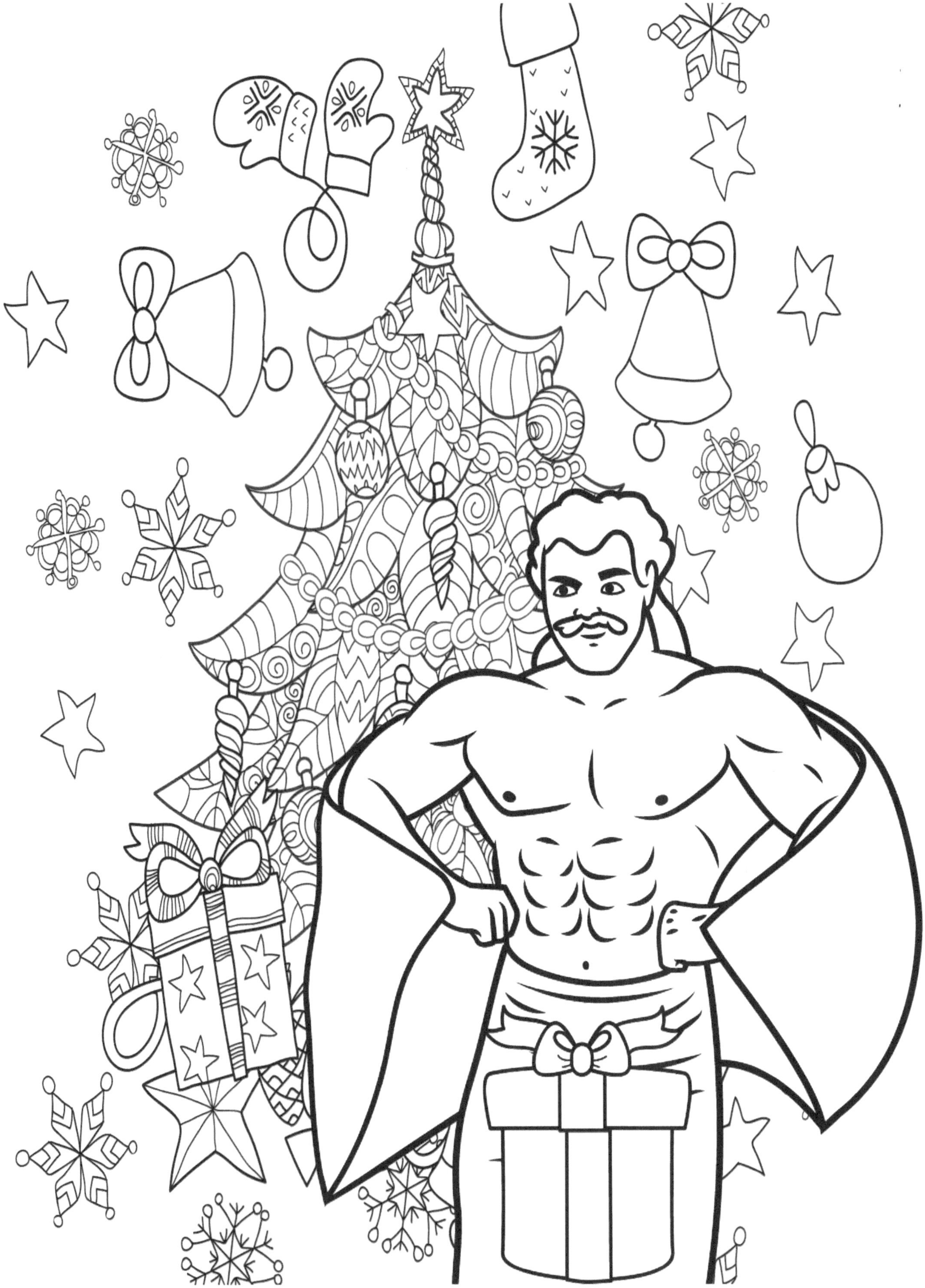

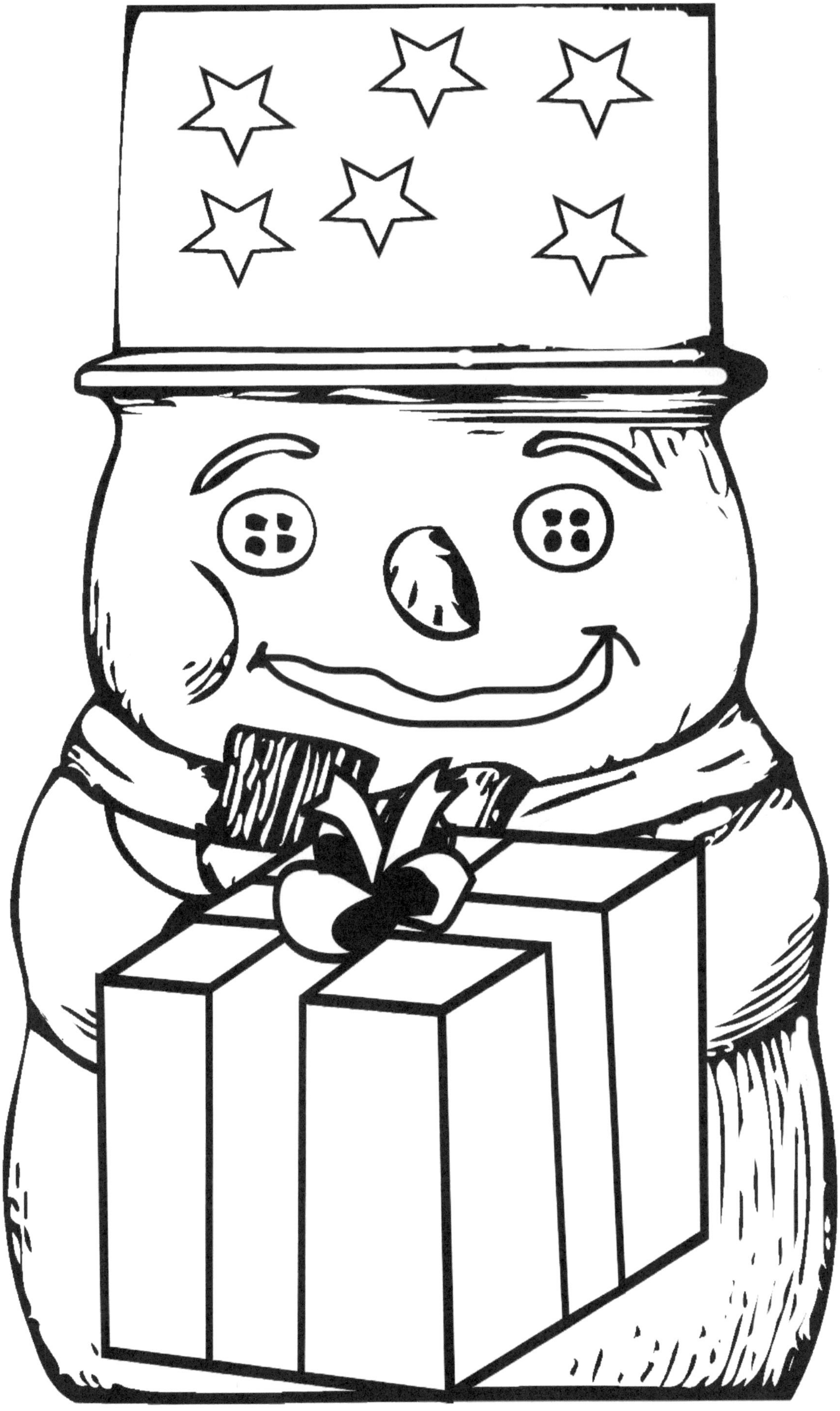

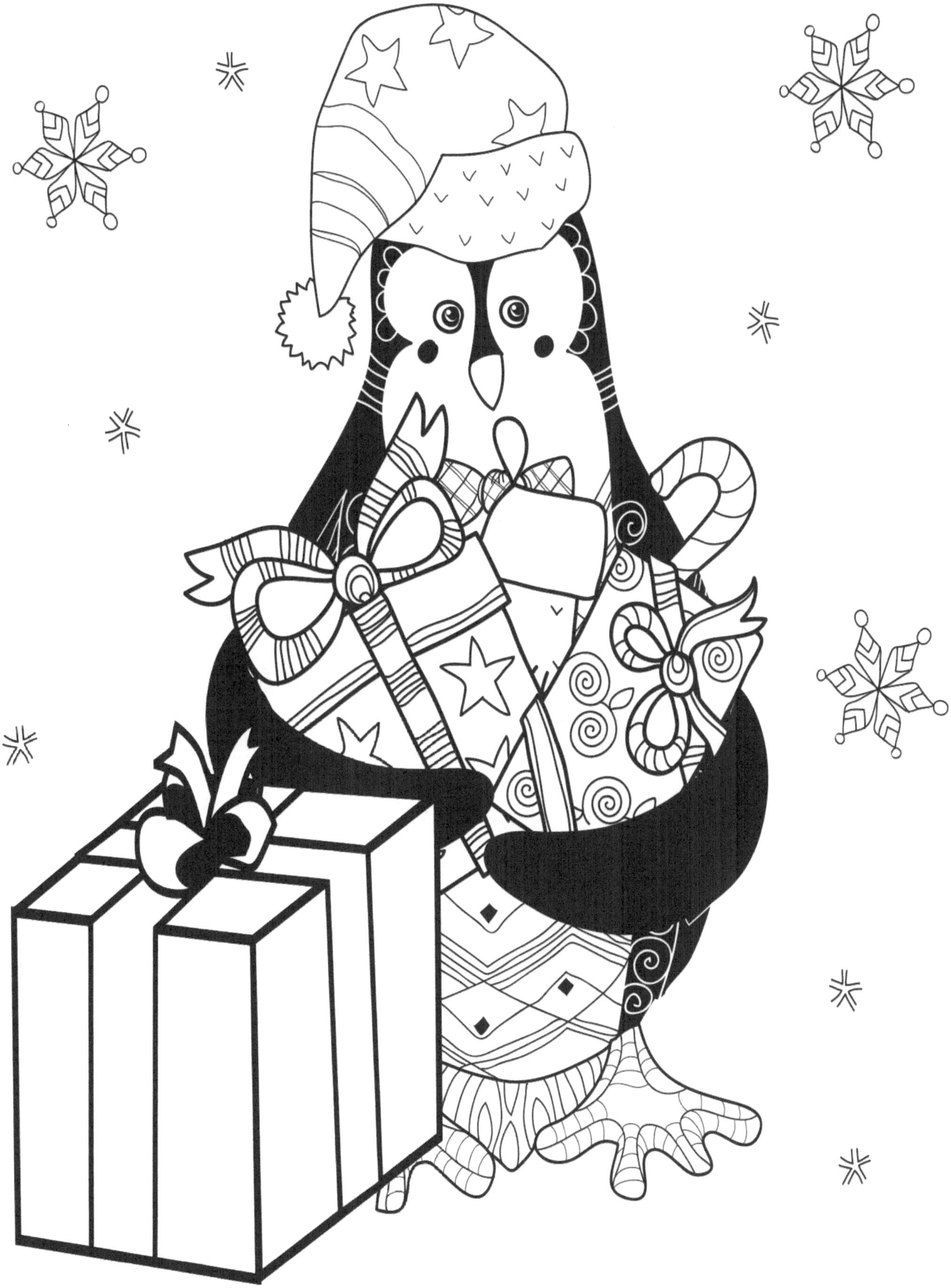

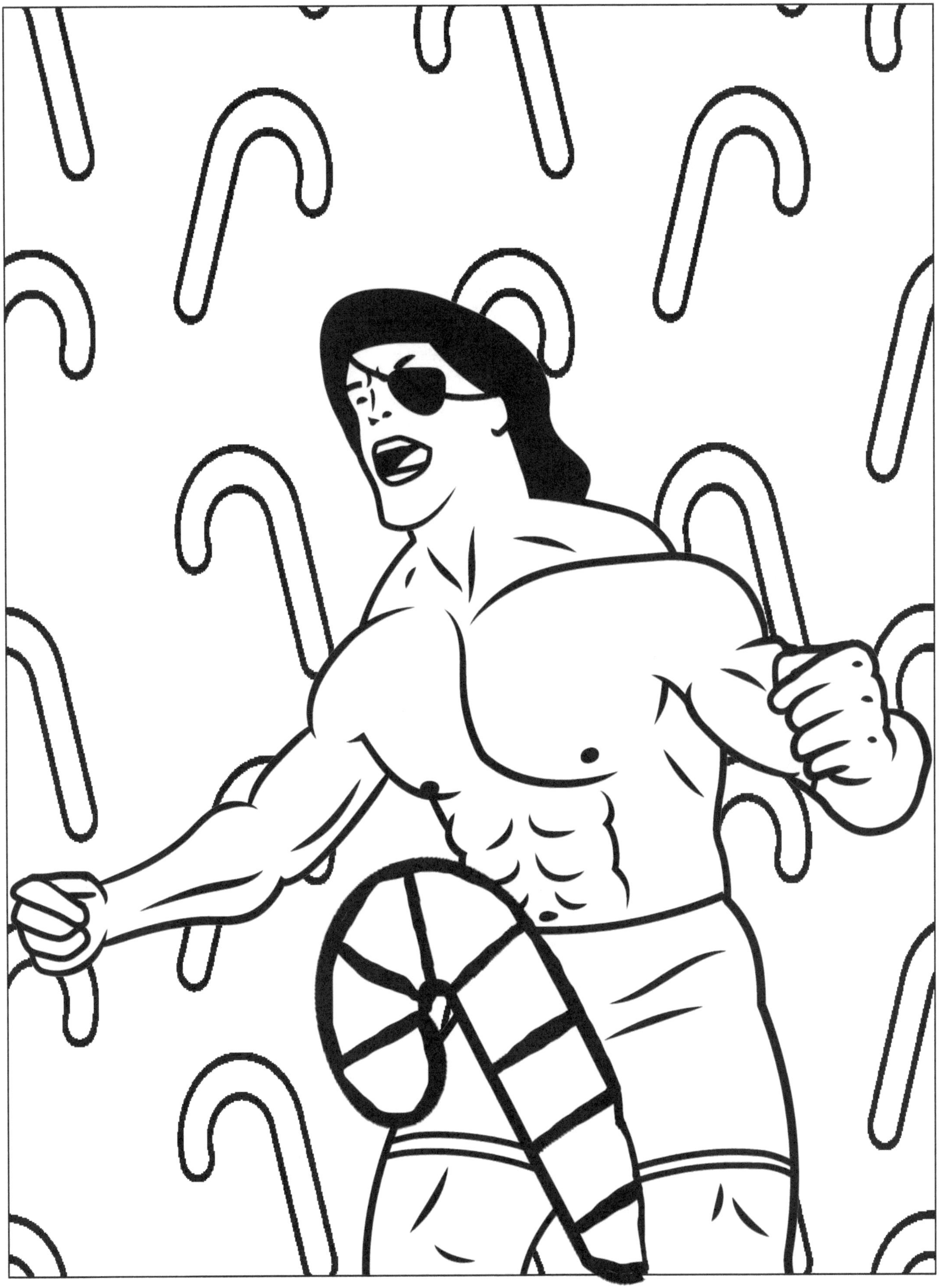

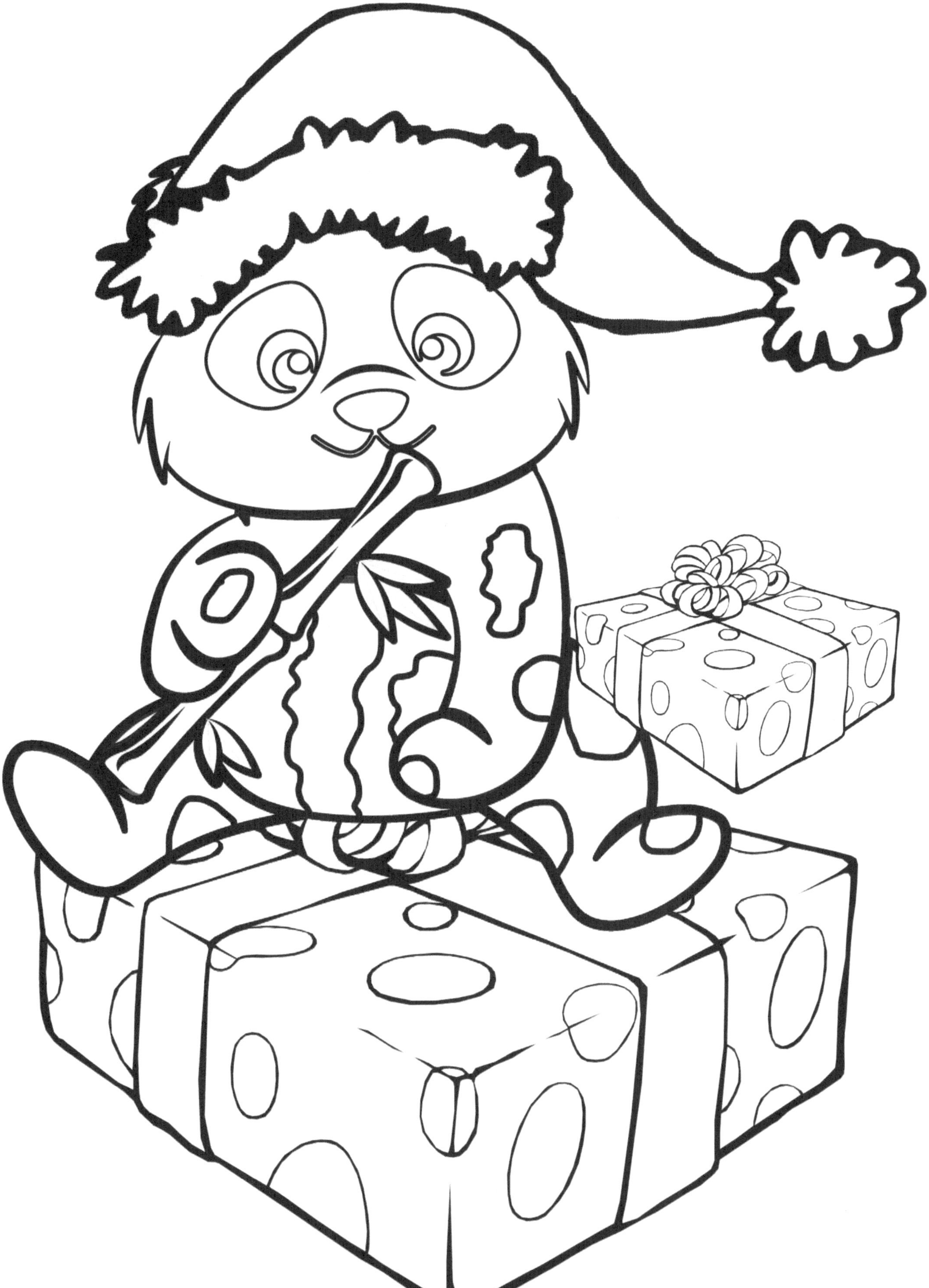

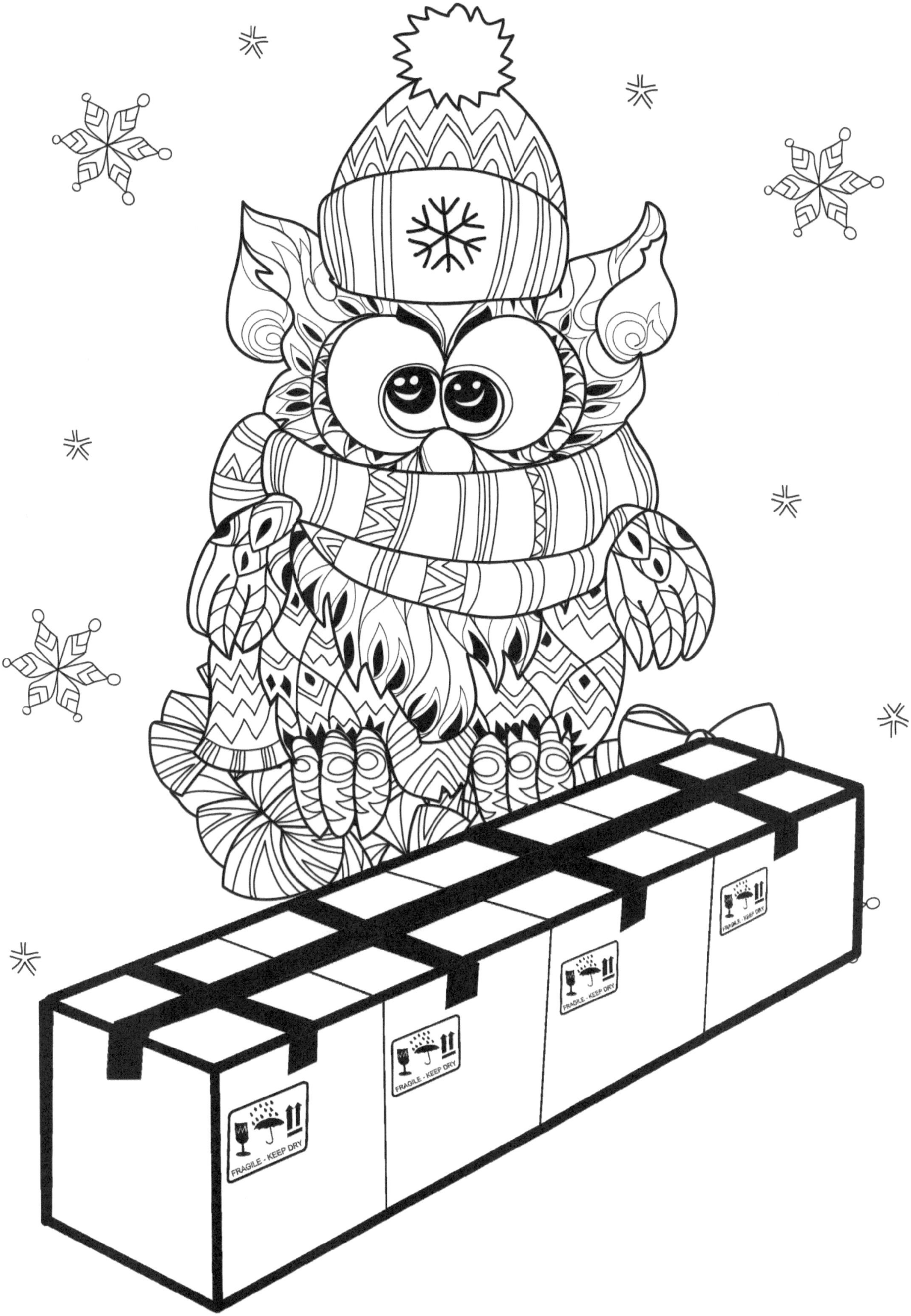
FRAGILE - KEEP DRY
FRAGILE - KEEP DRY
FRAGILE - KEEP DRY
FRAGILE - KEEP DRY

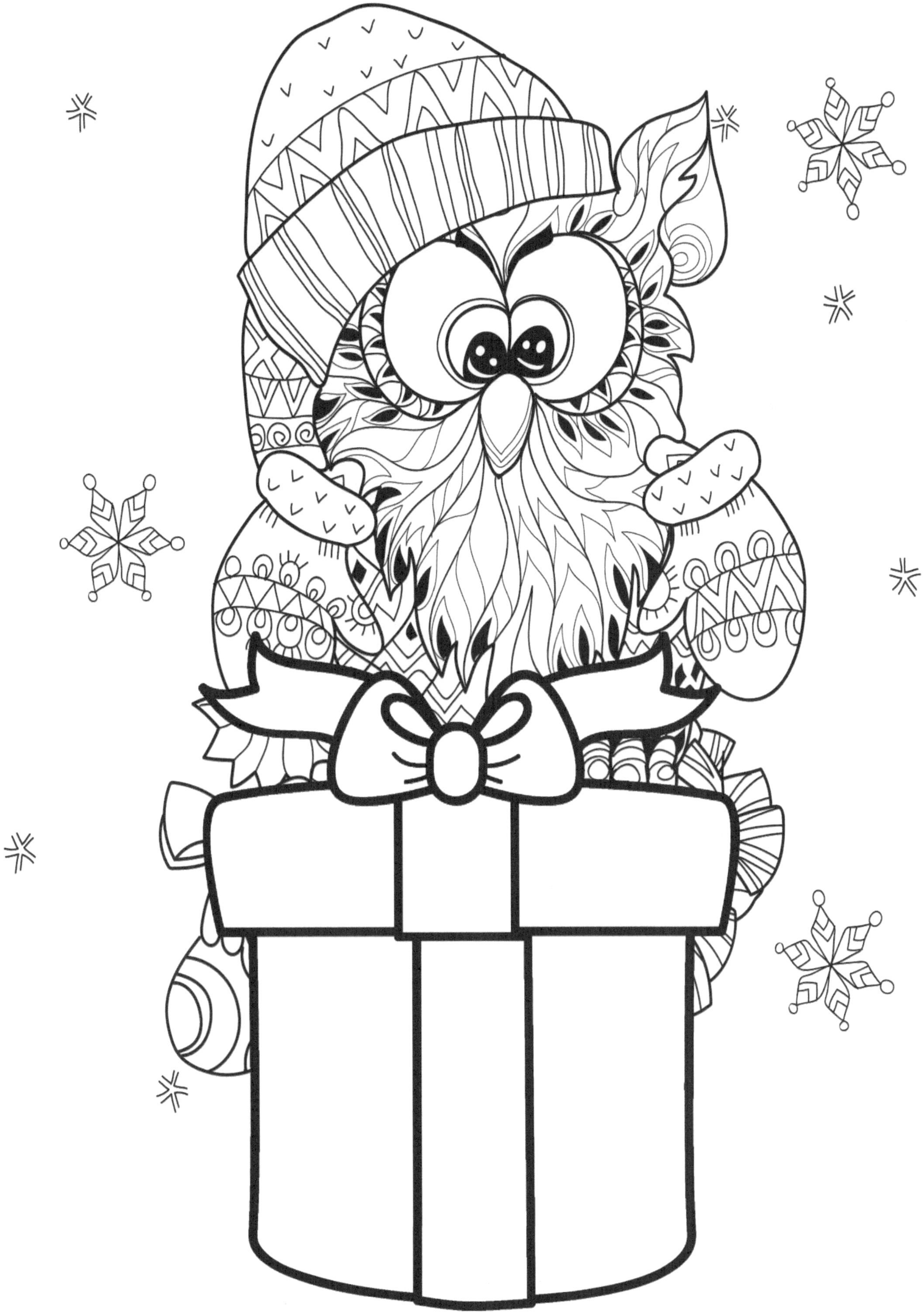

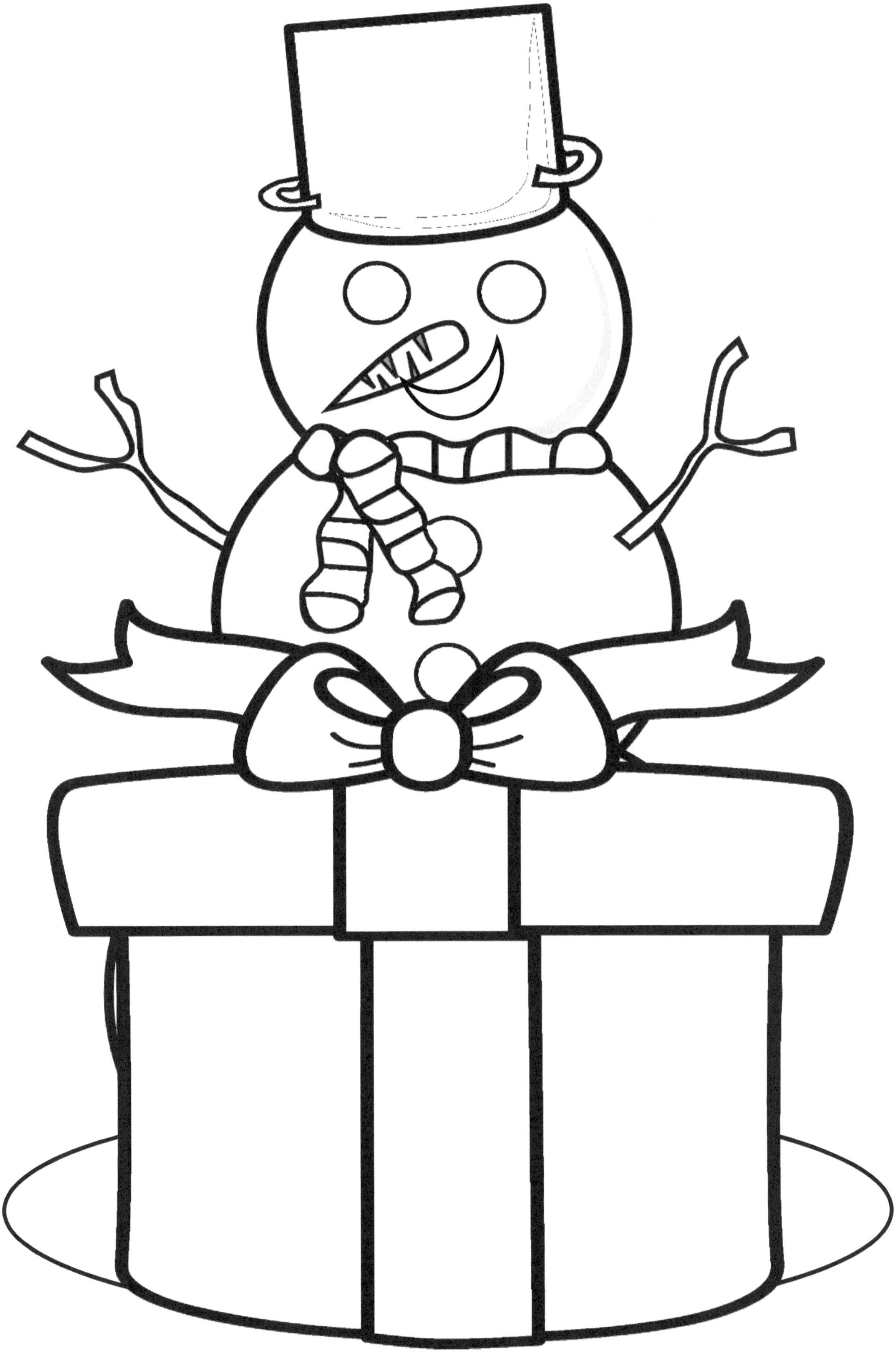

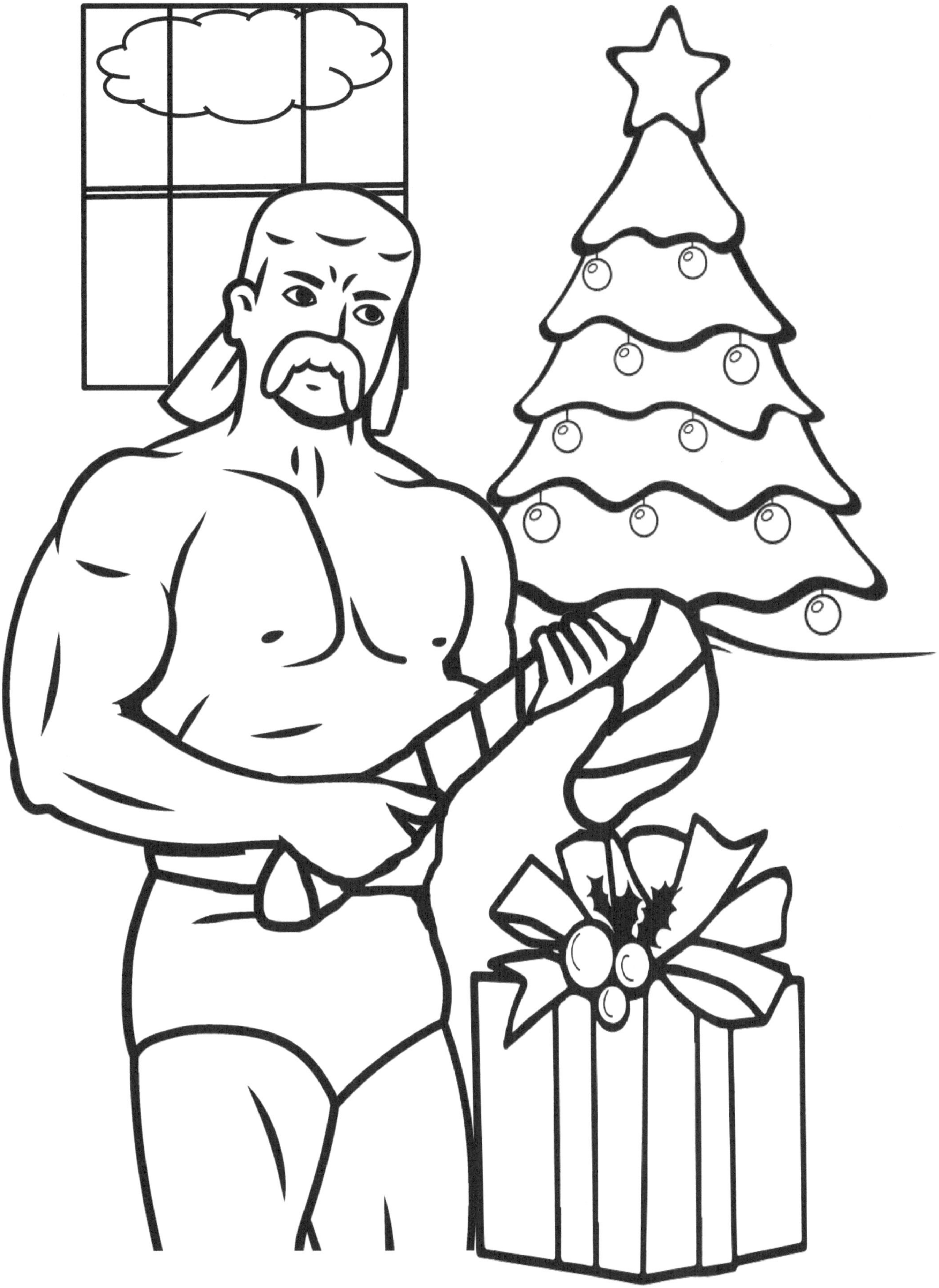

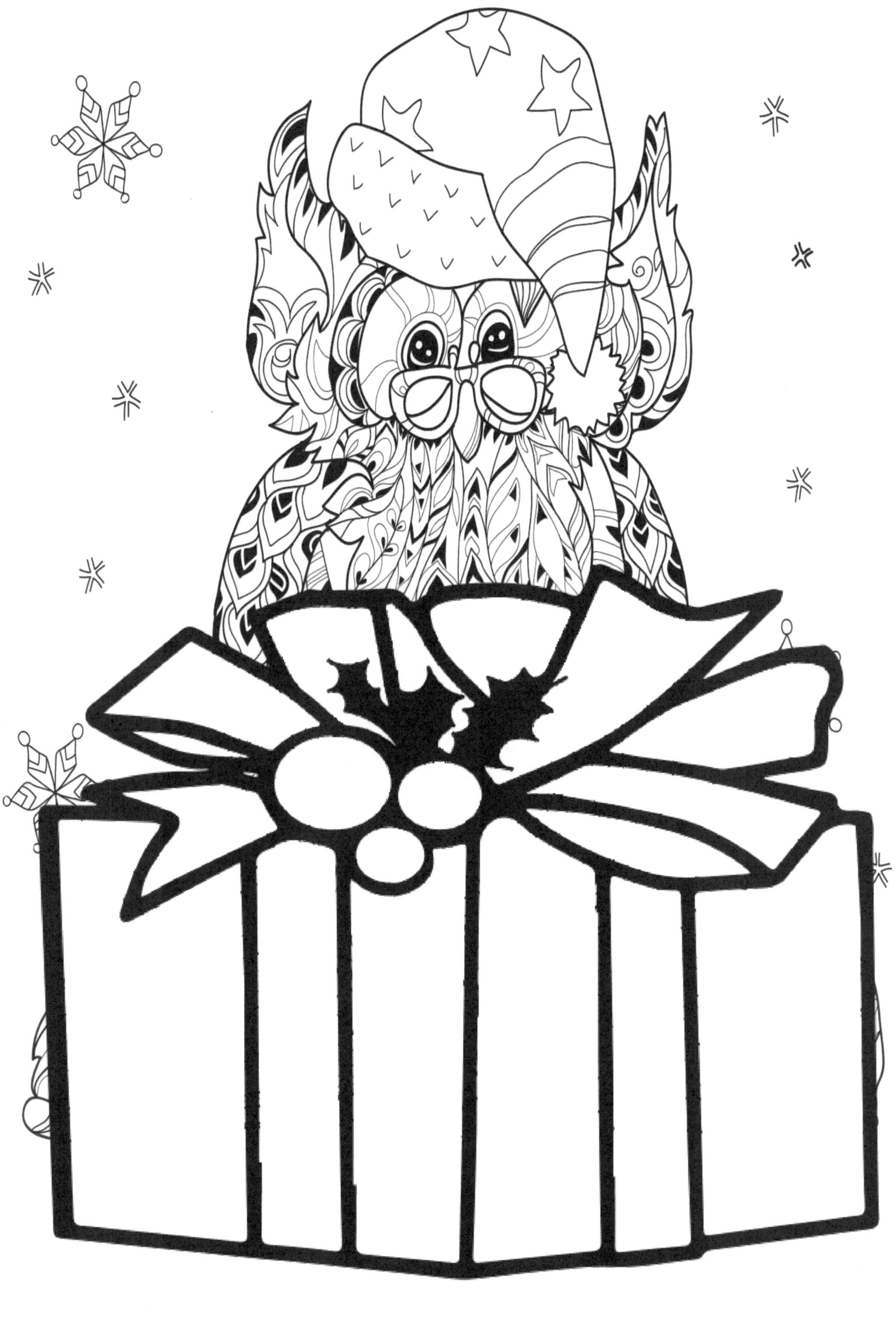

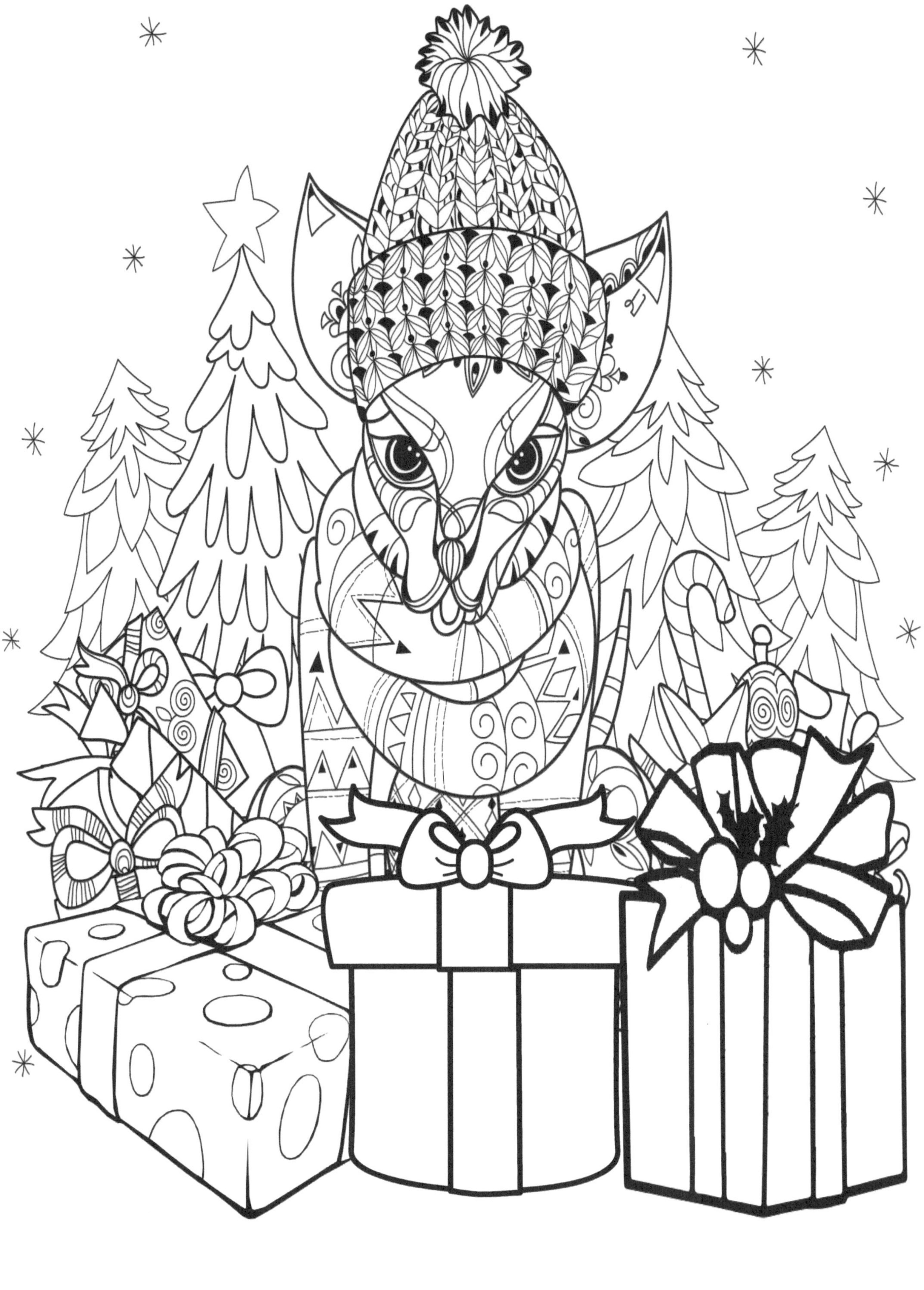

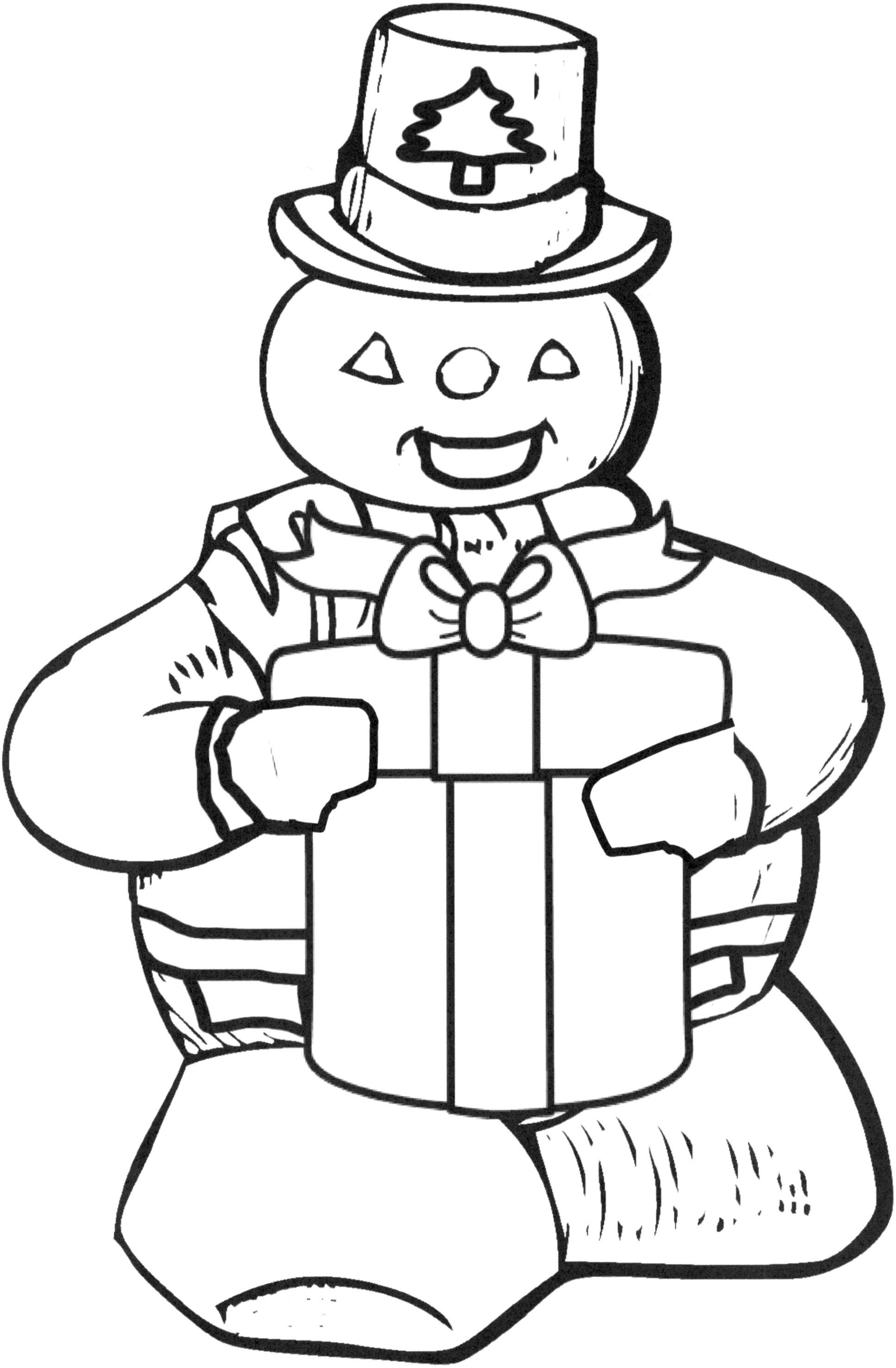

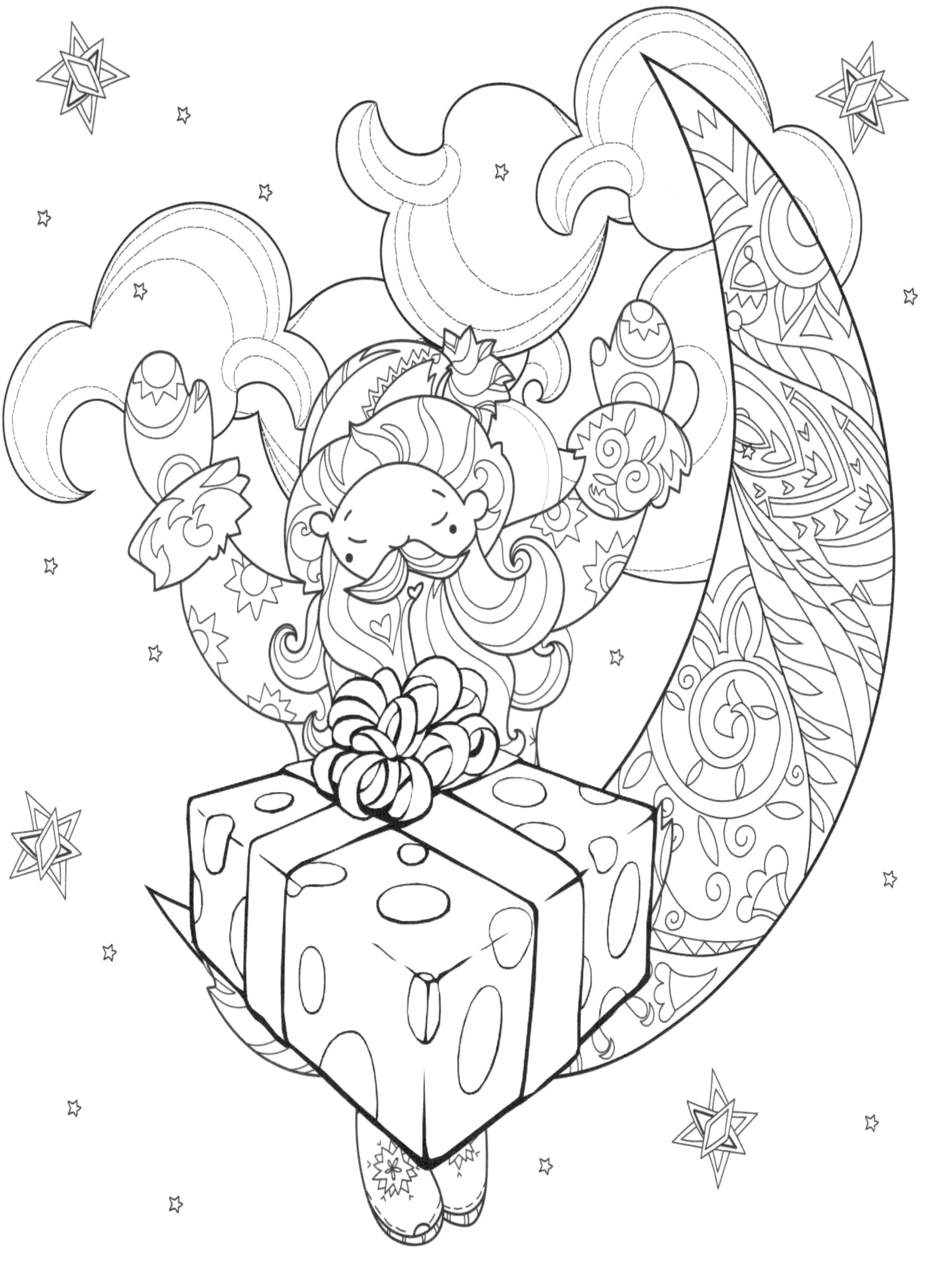

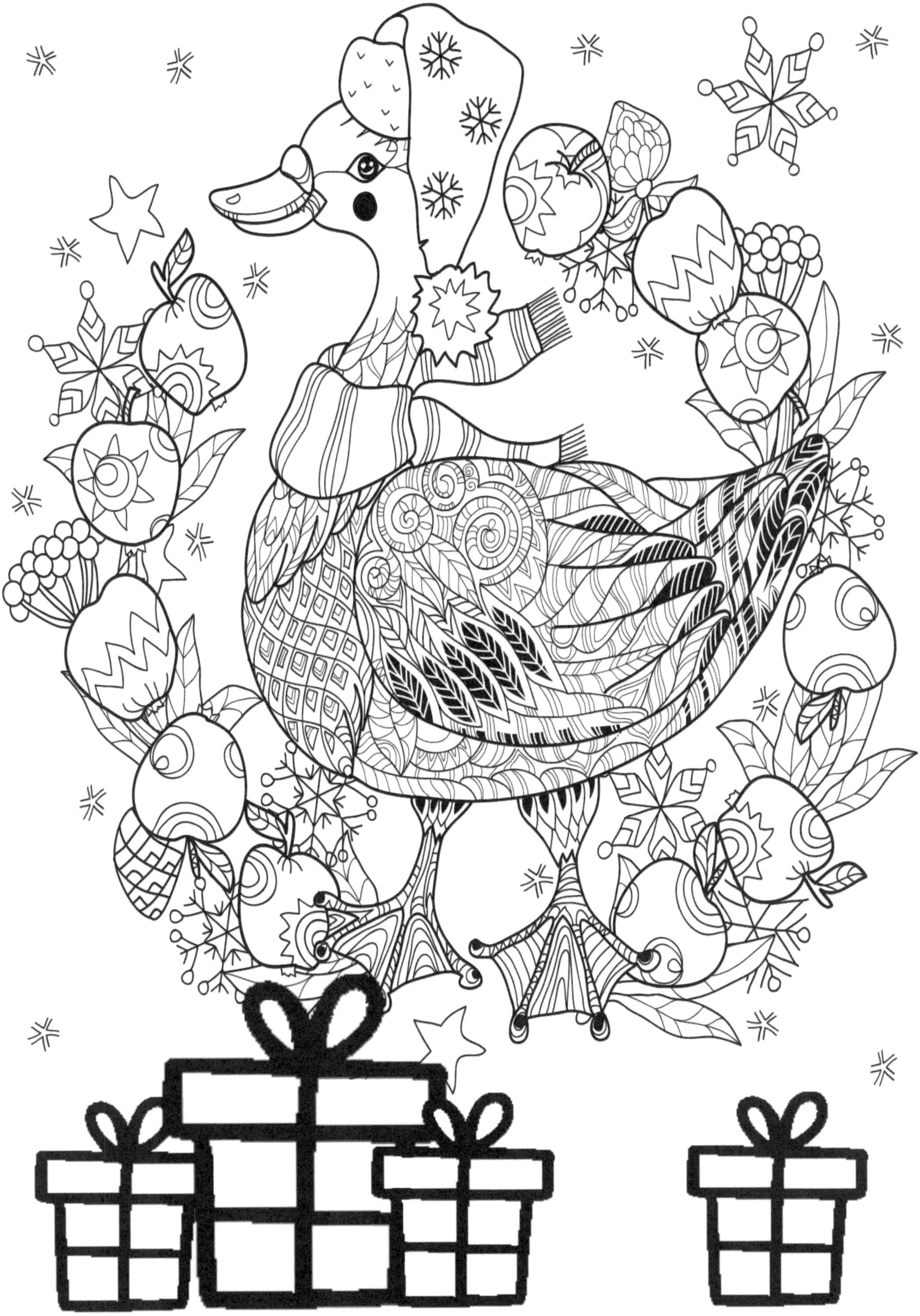

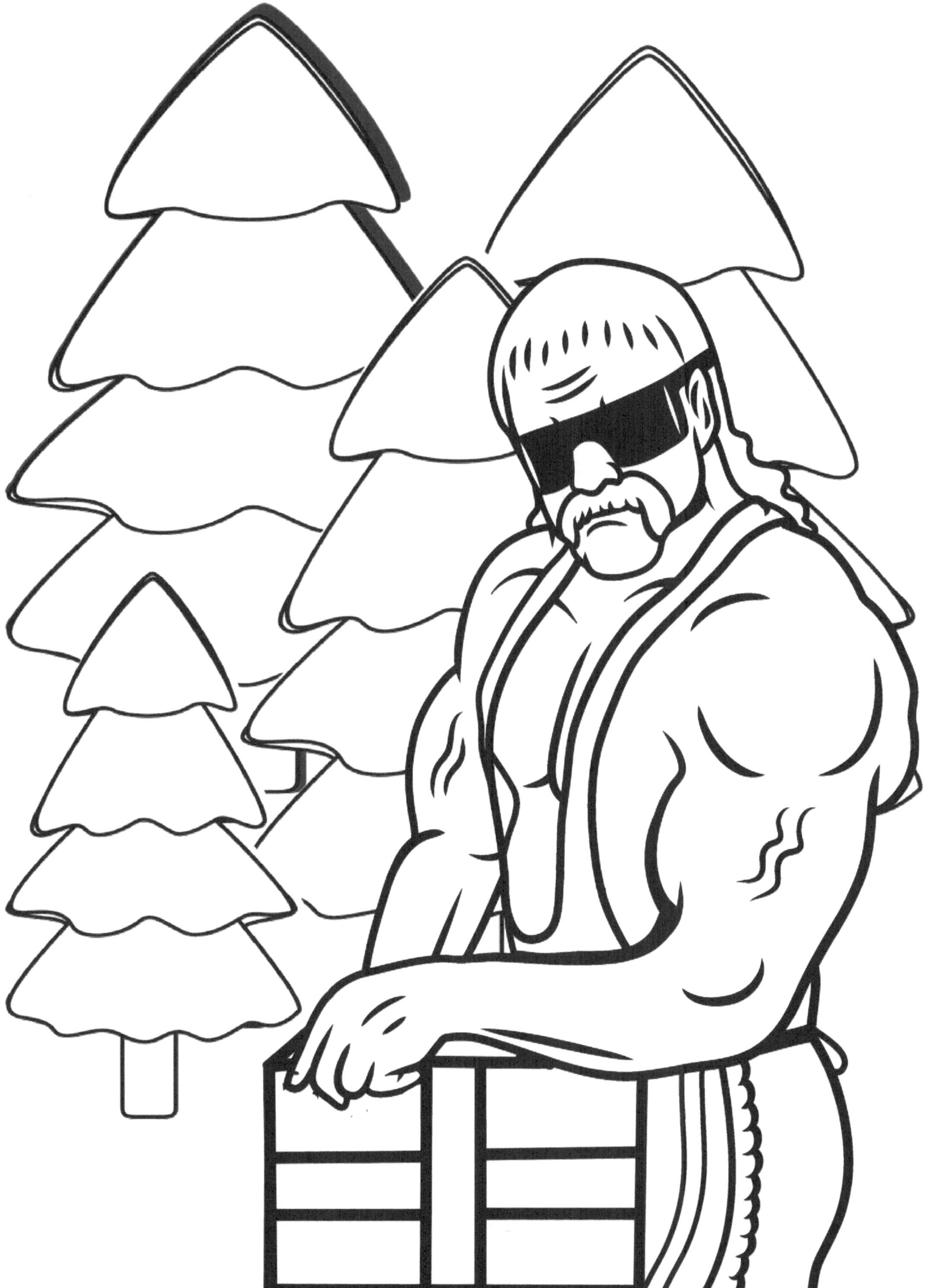

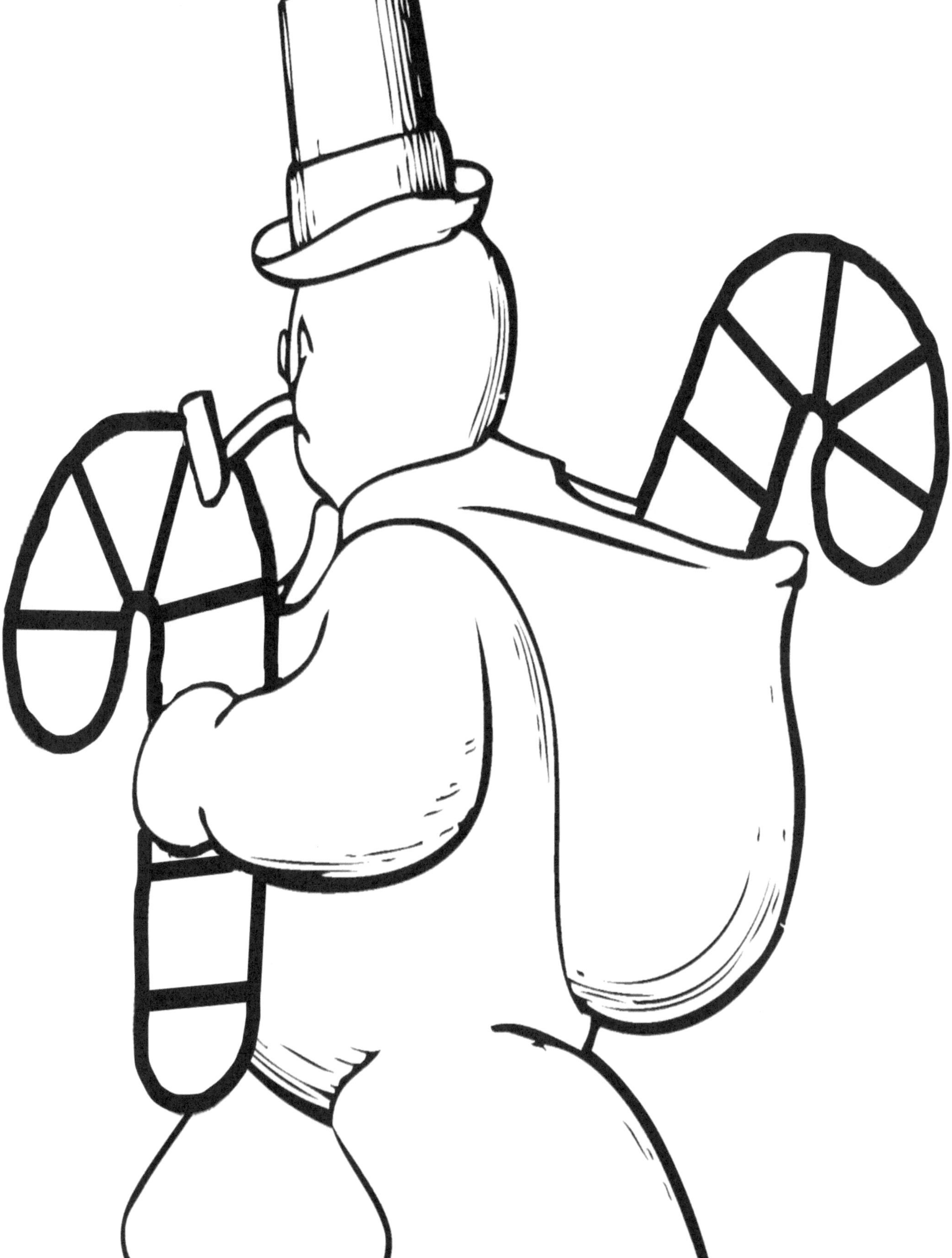

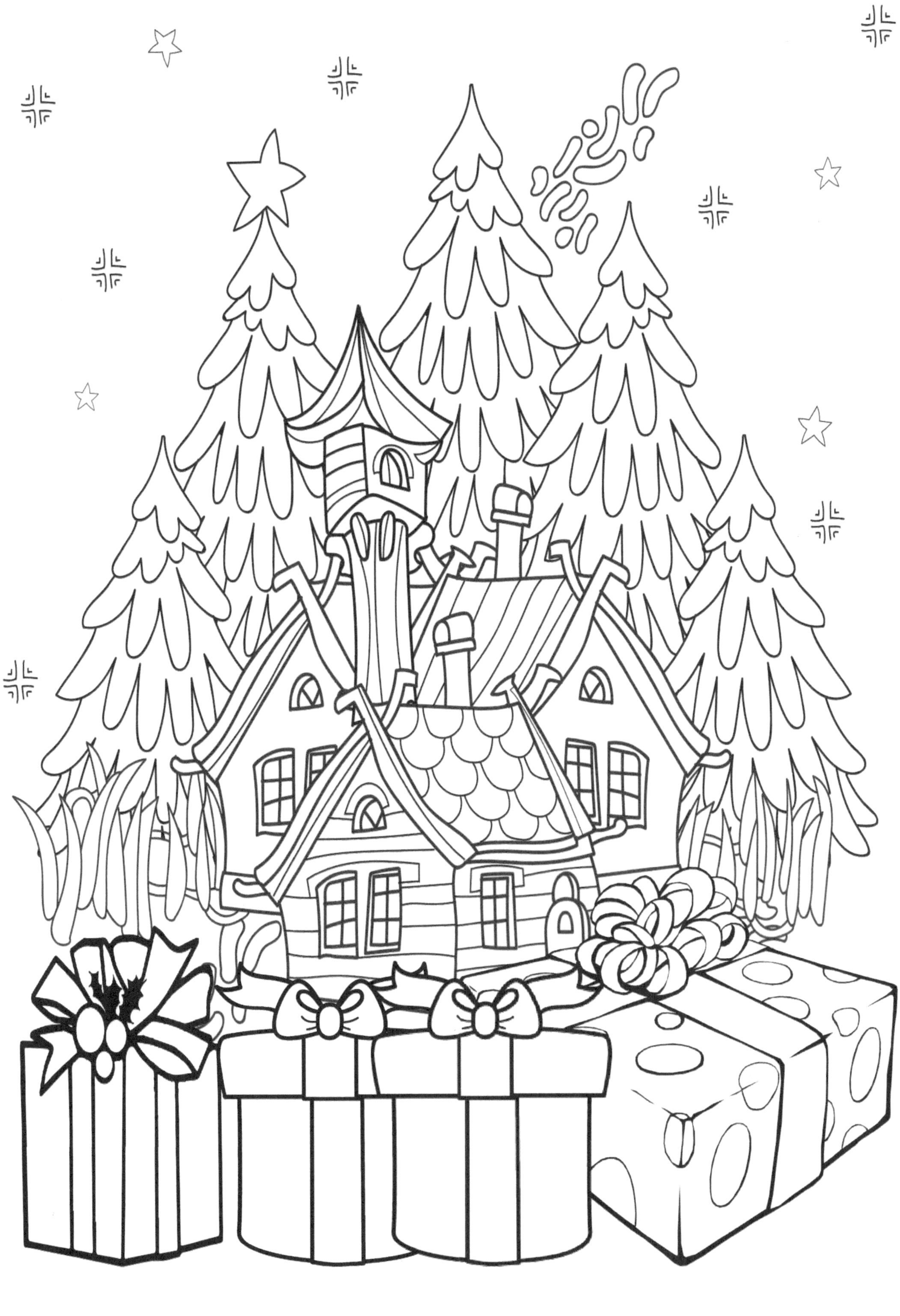

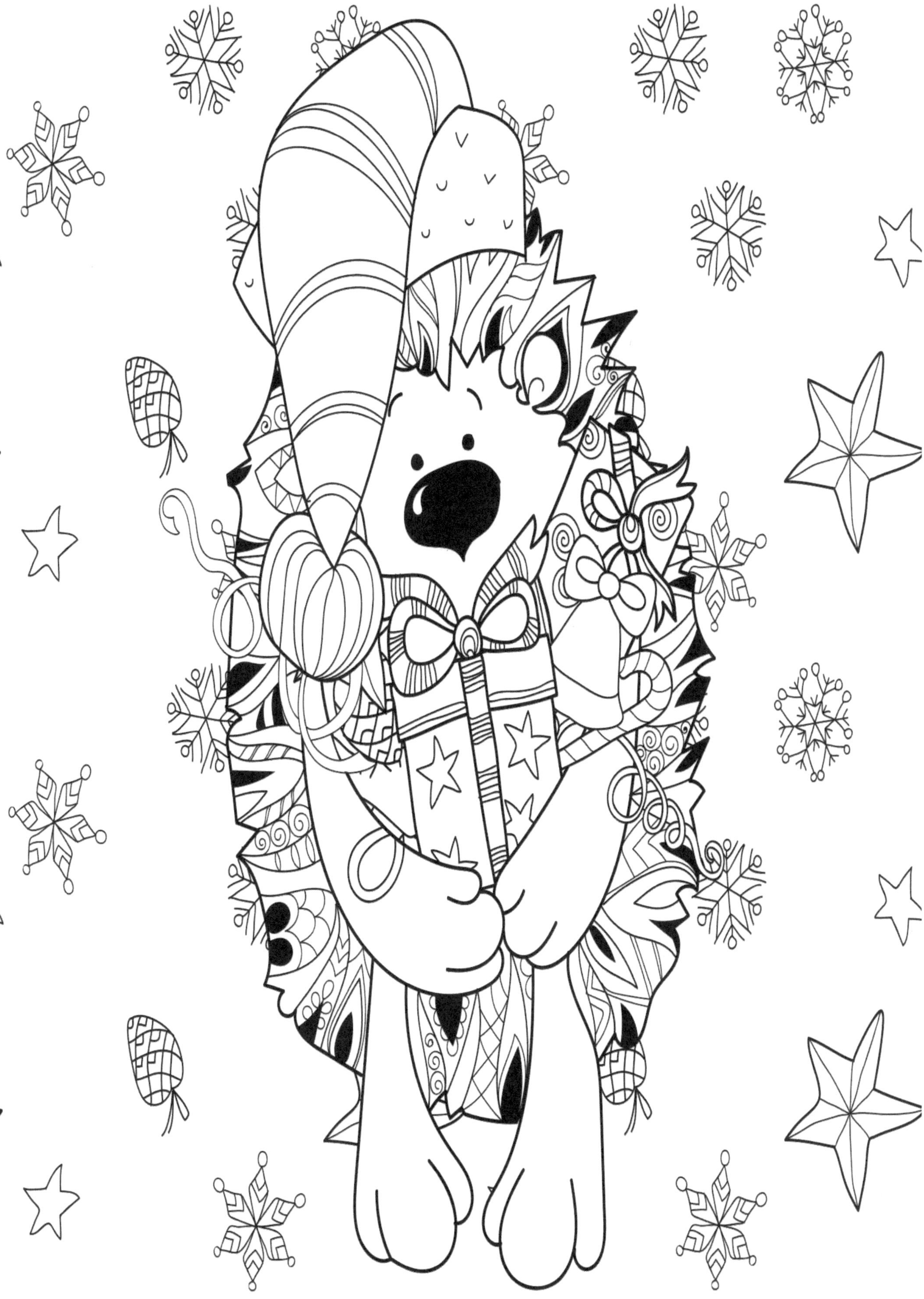

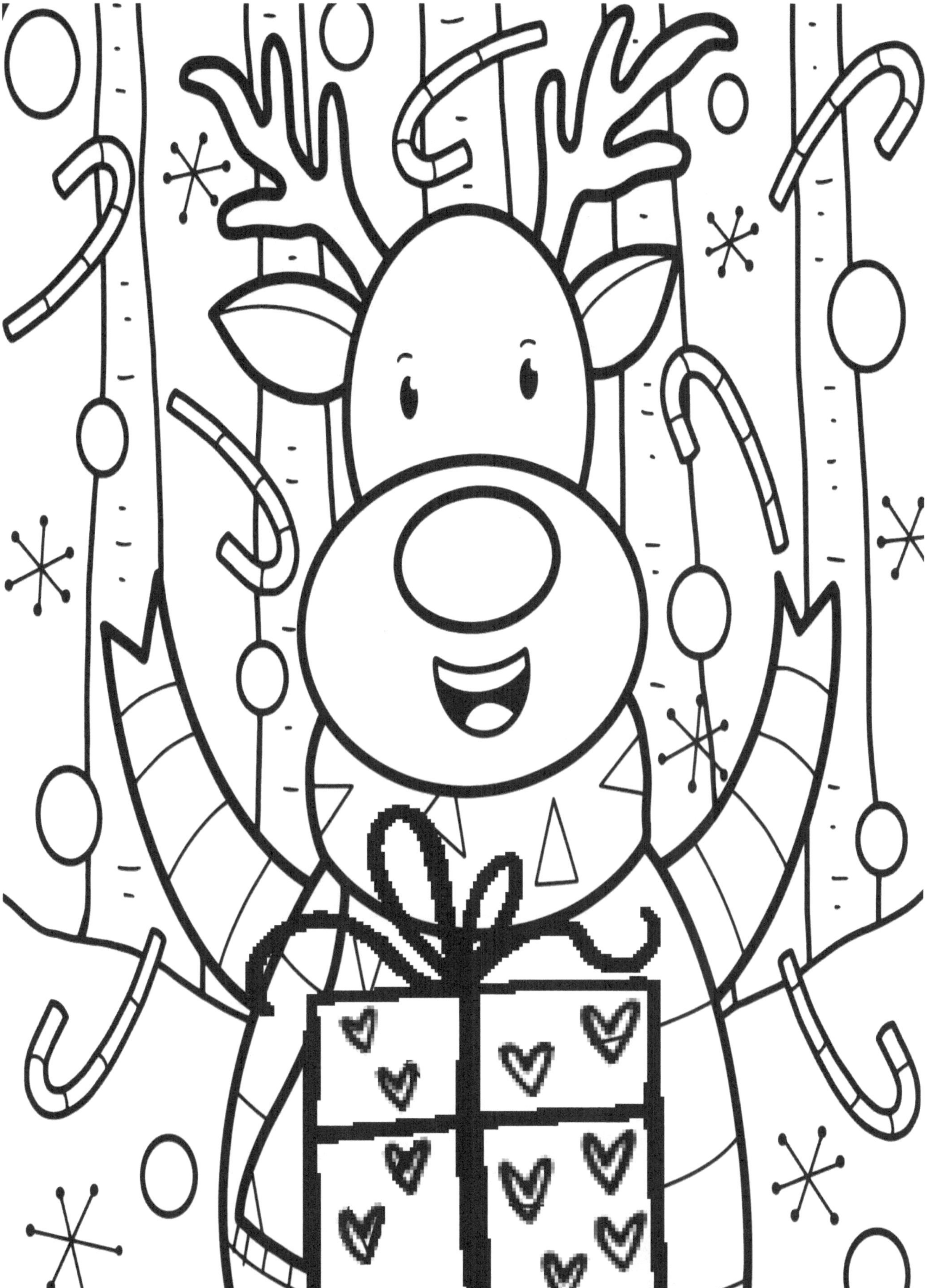

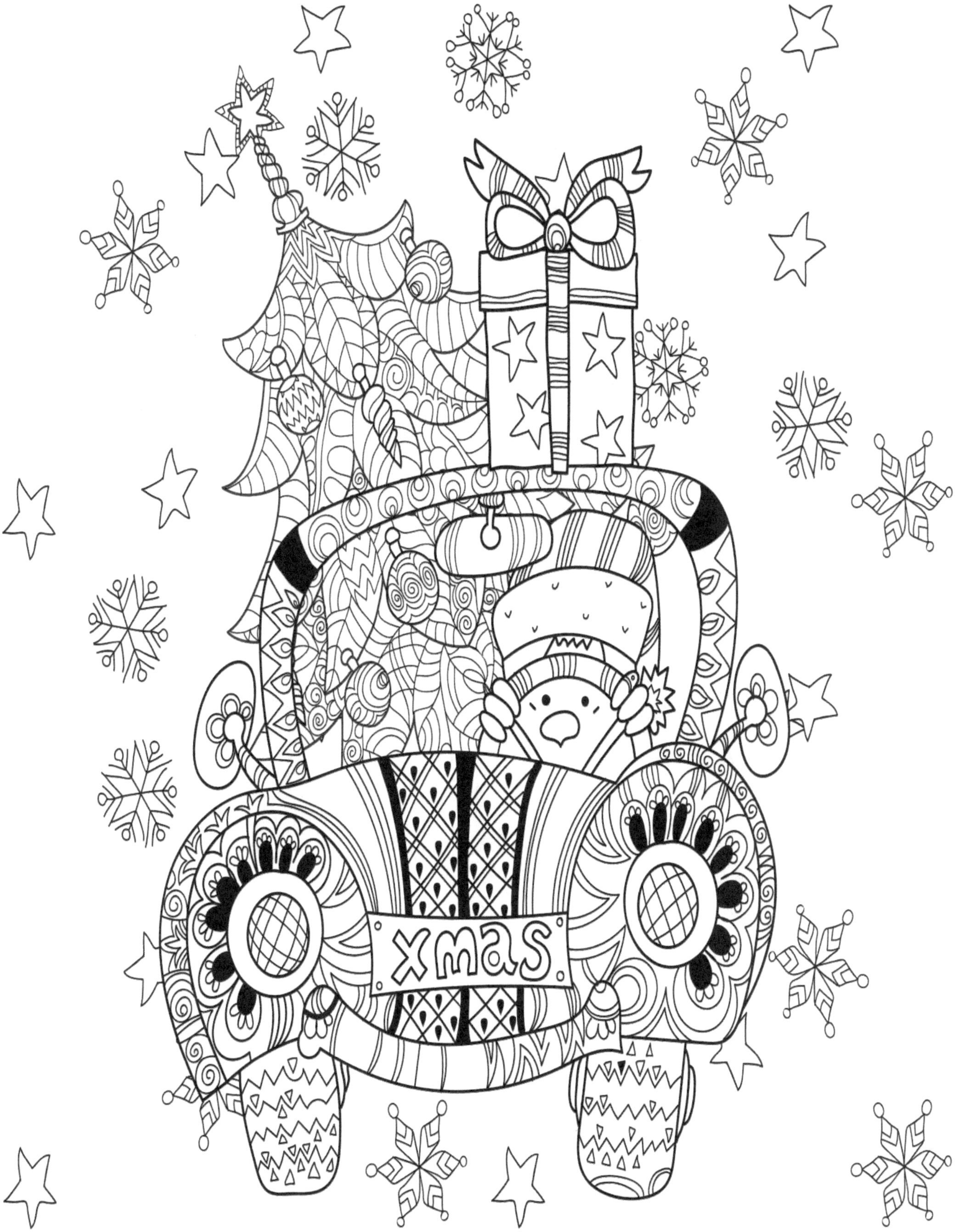
xmas

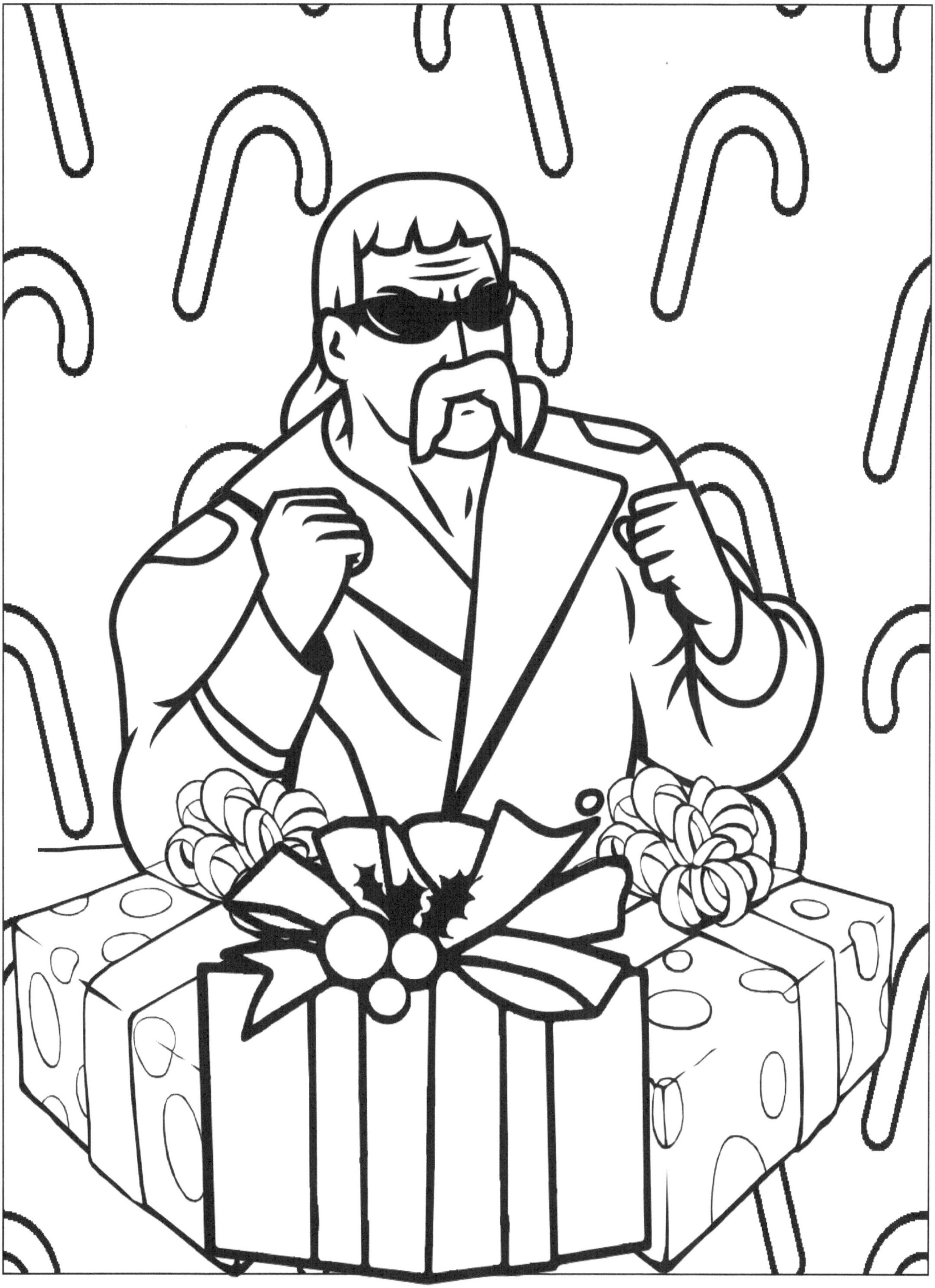

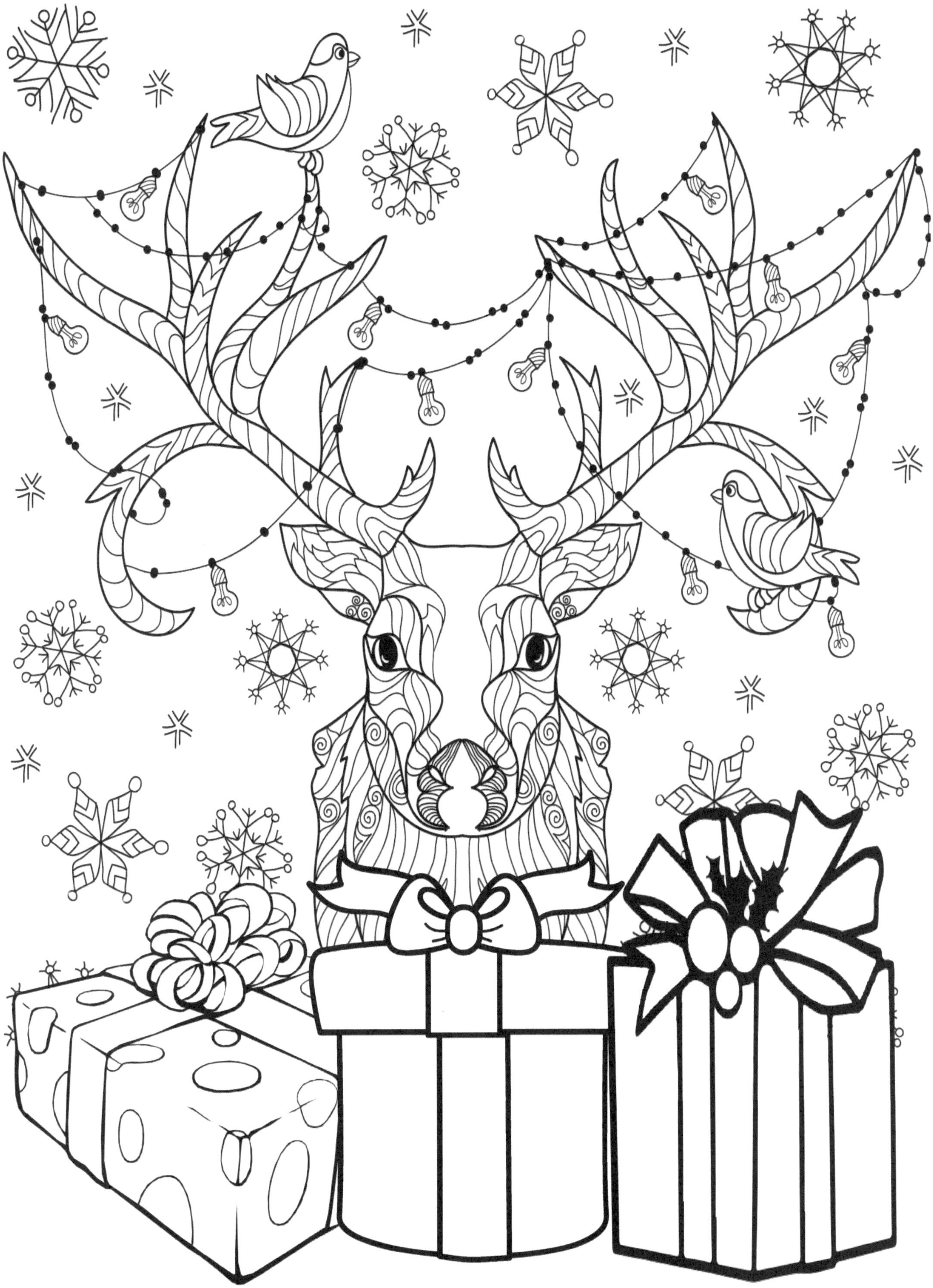

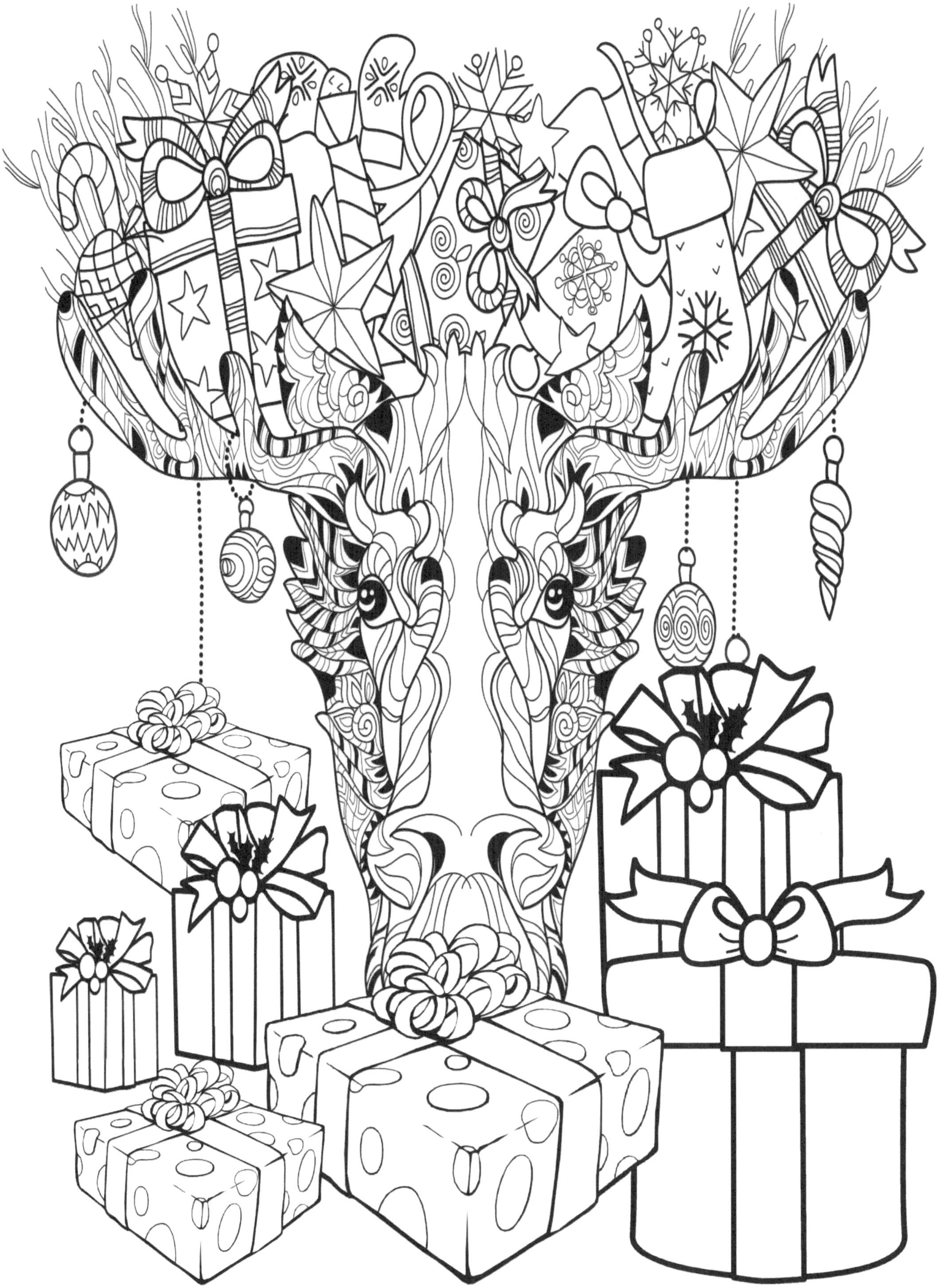

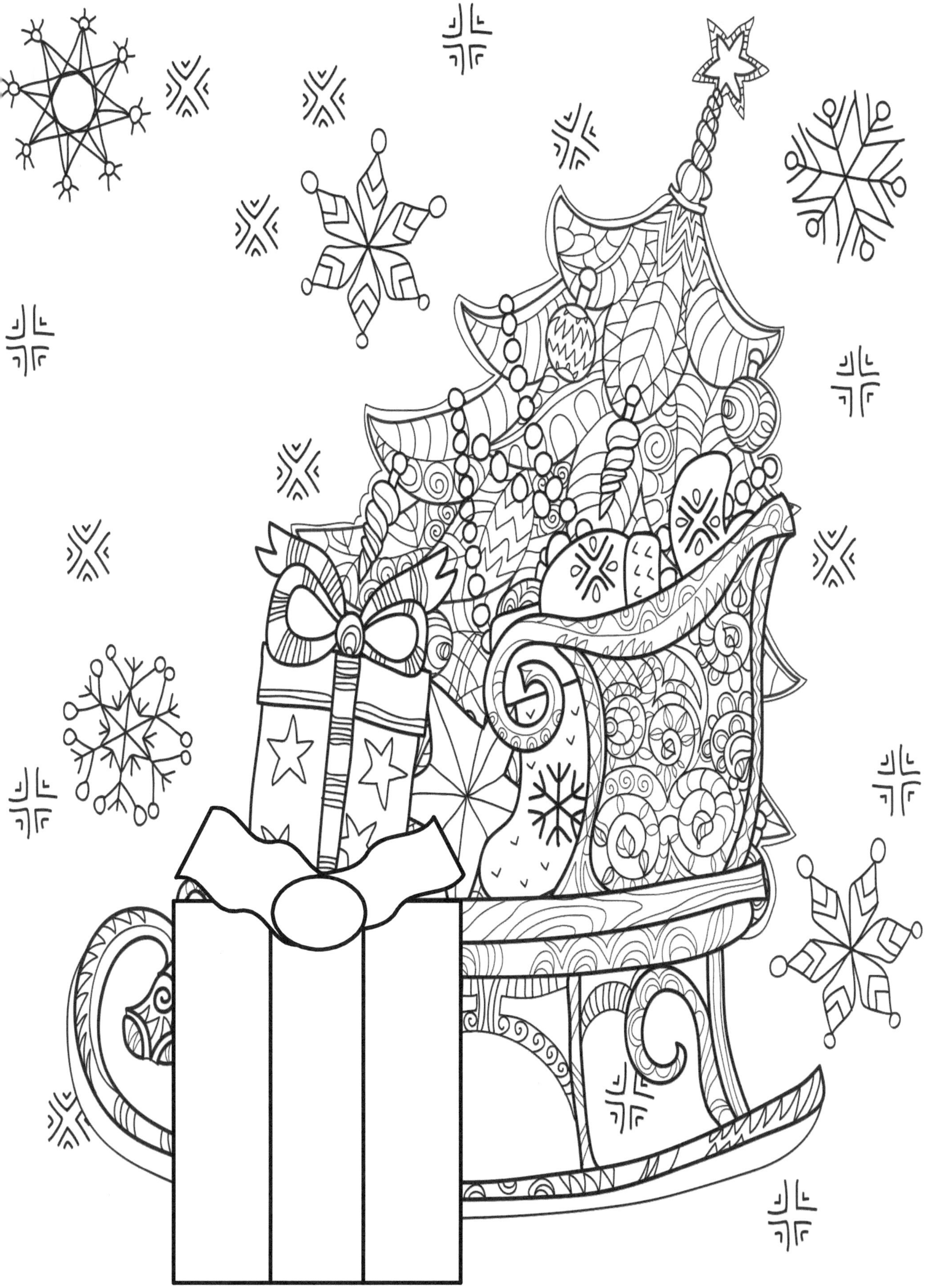

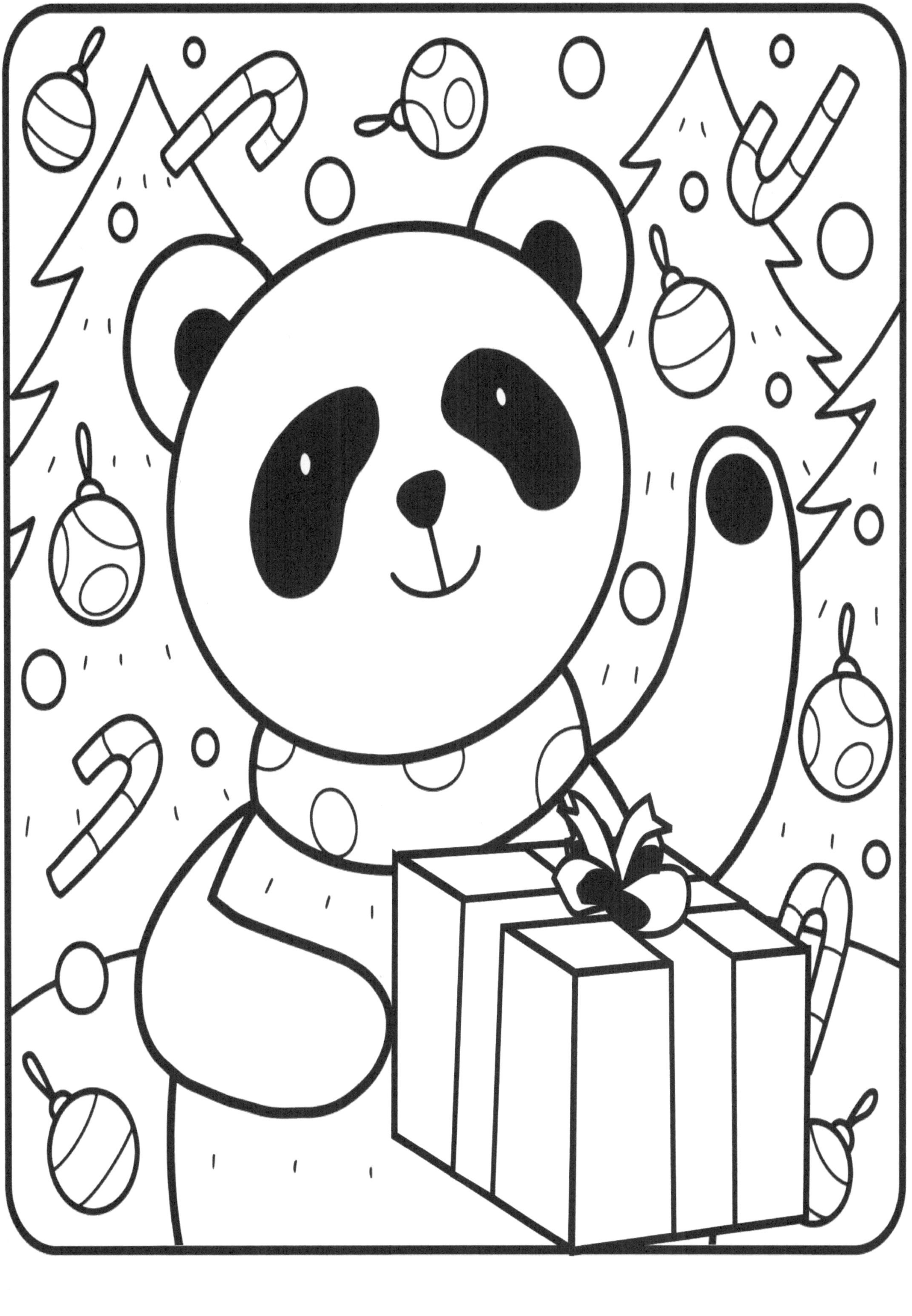

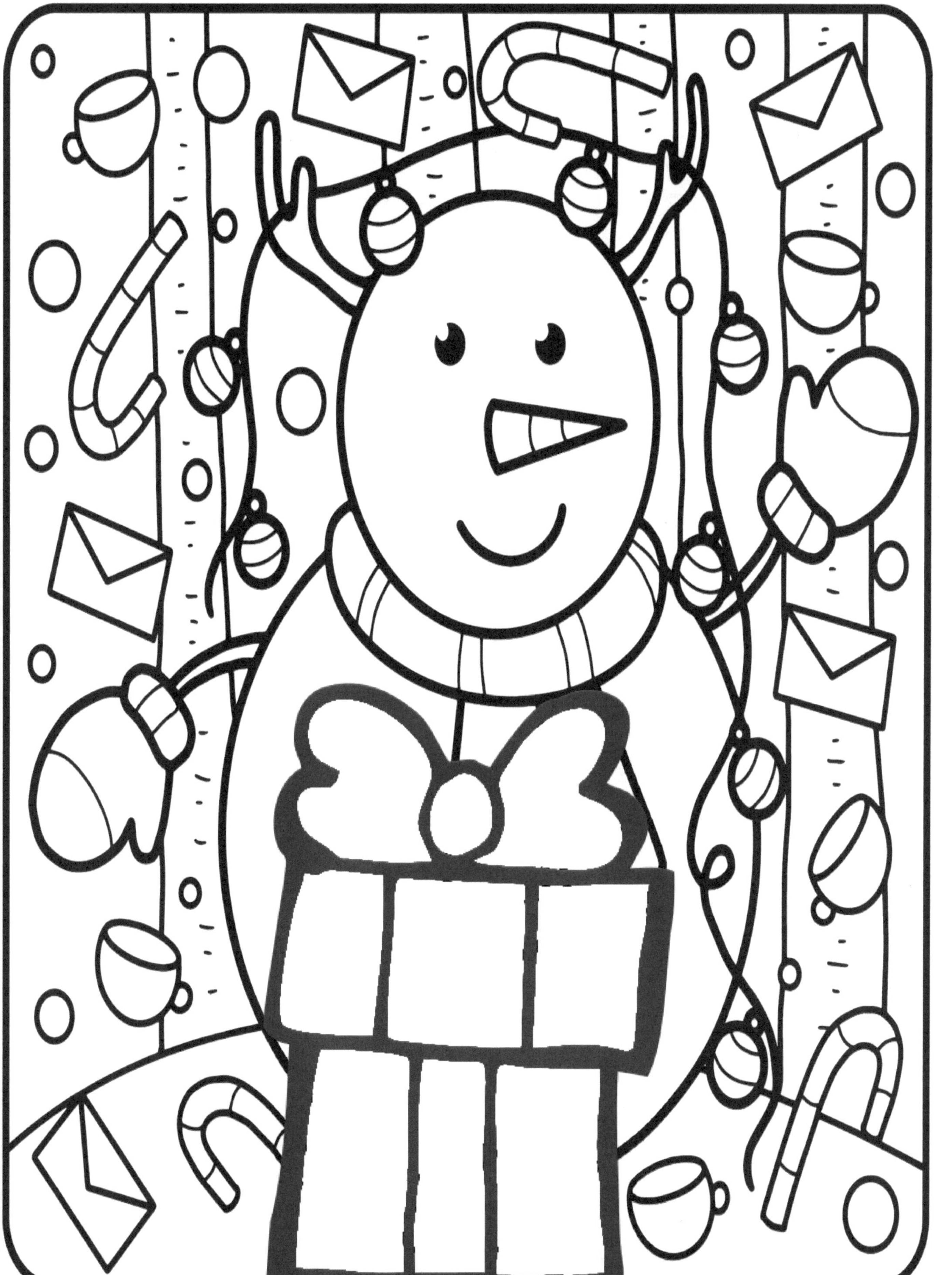

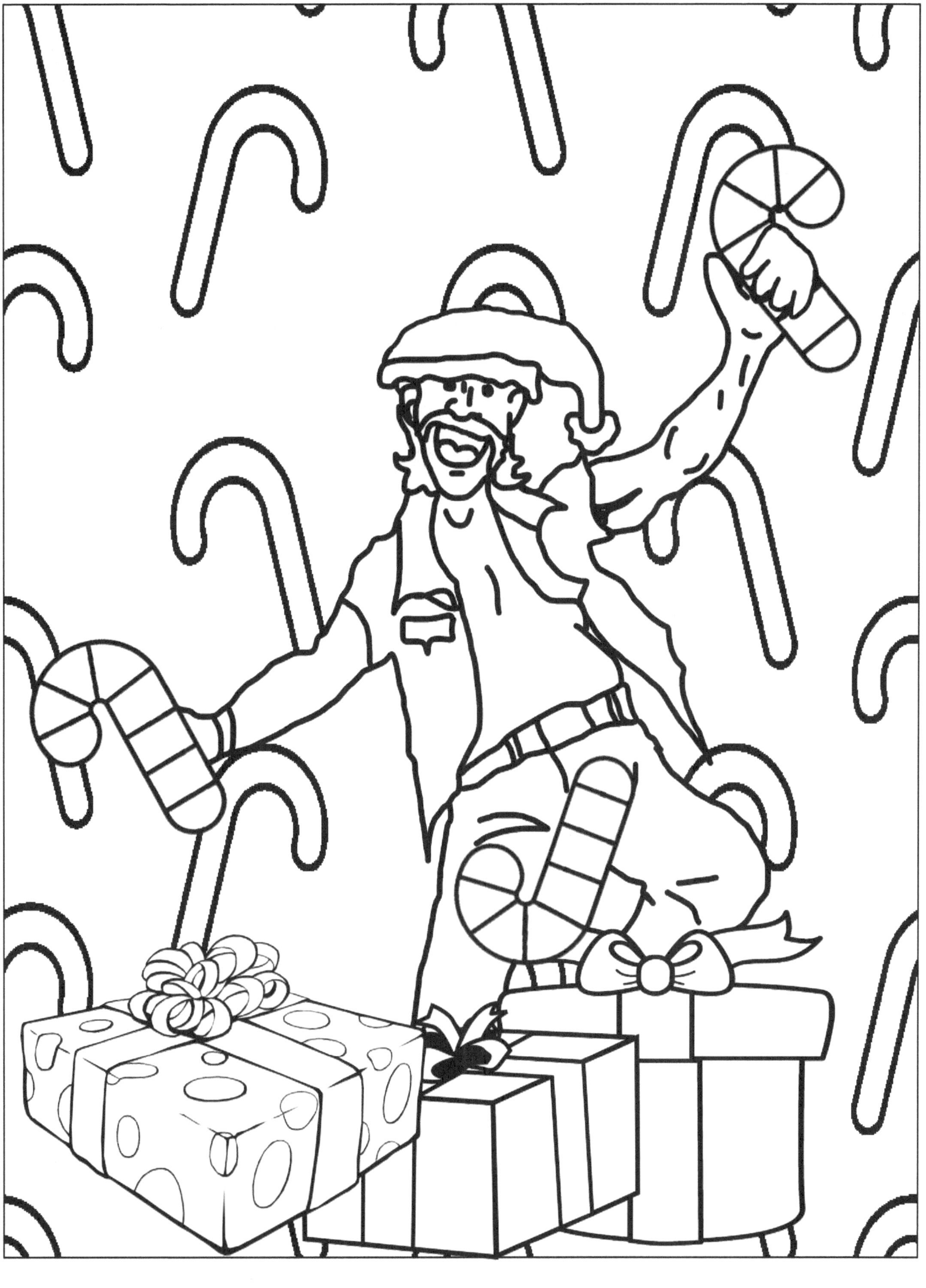

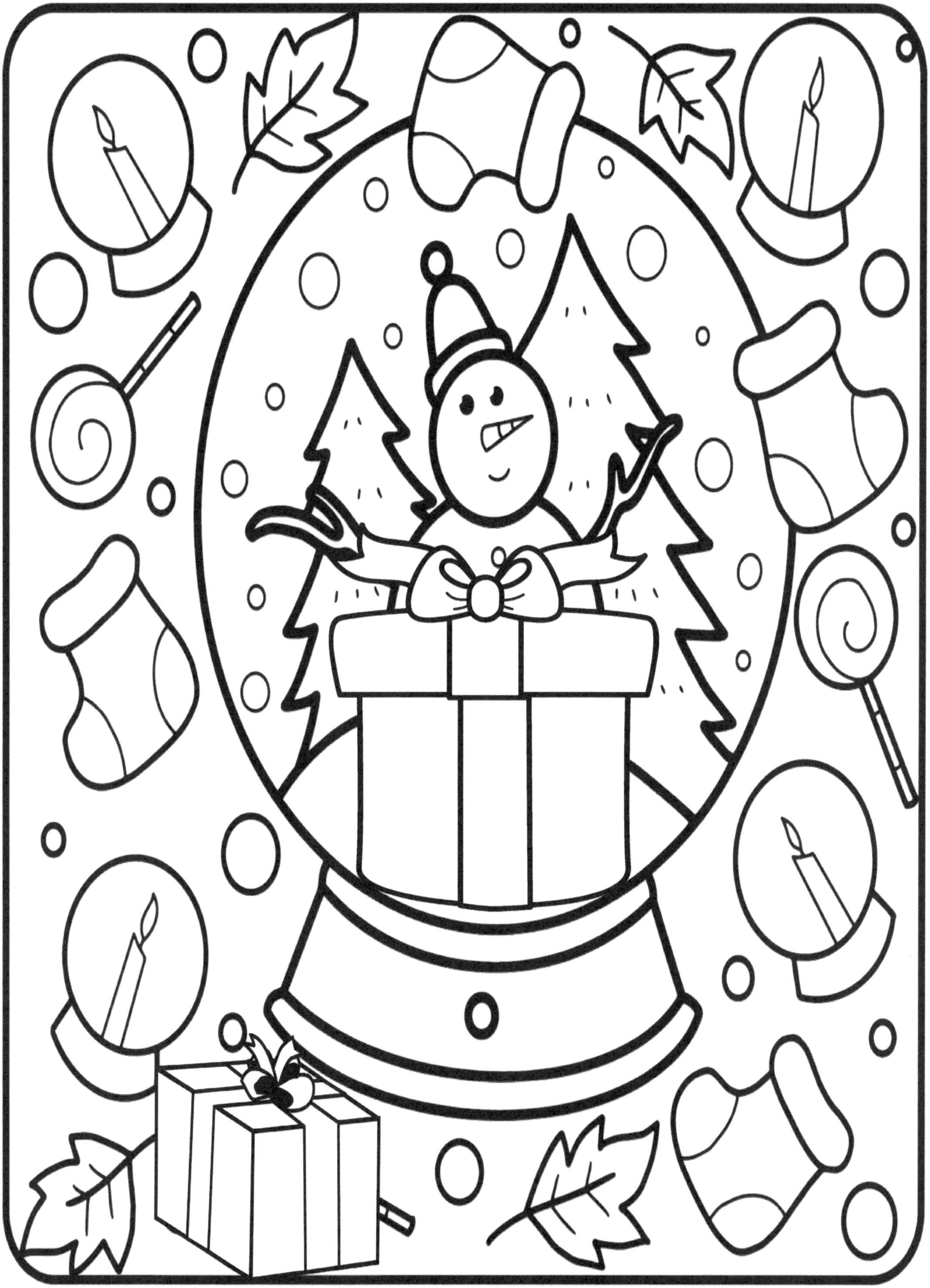

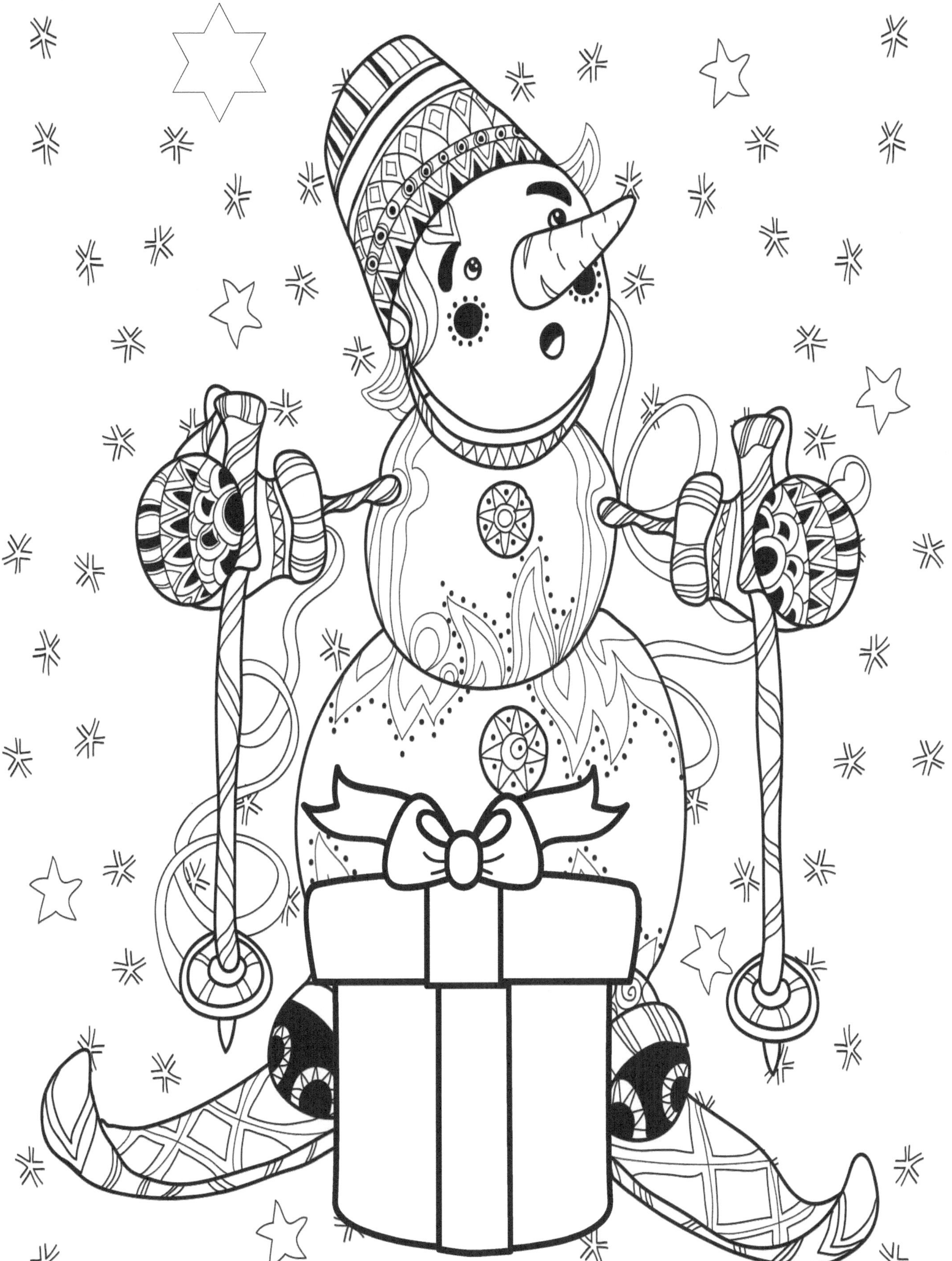

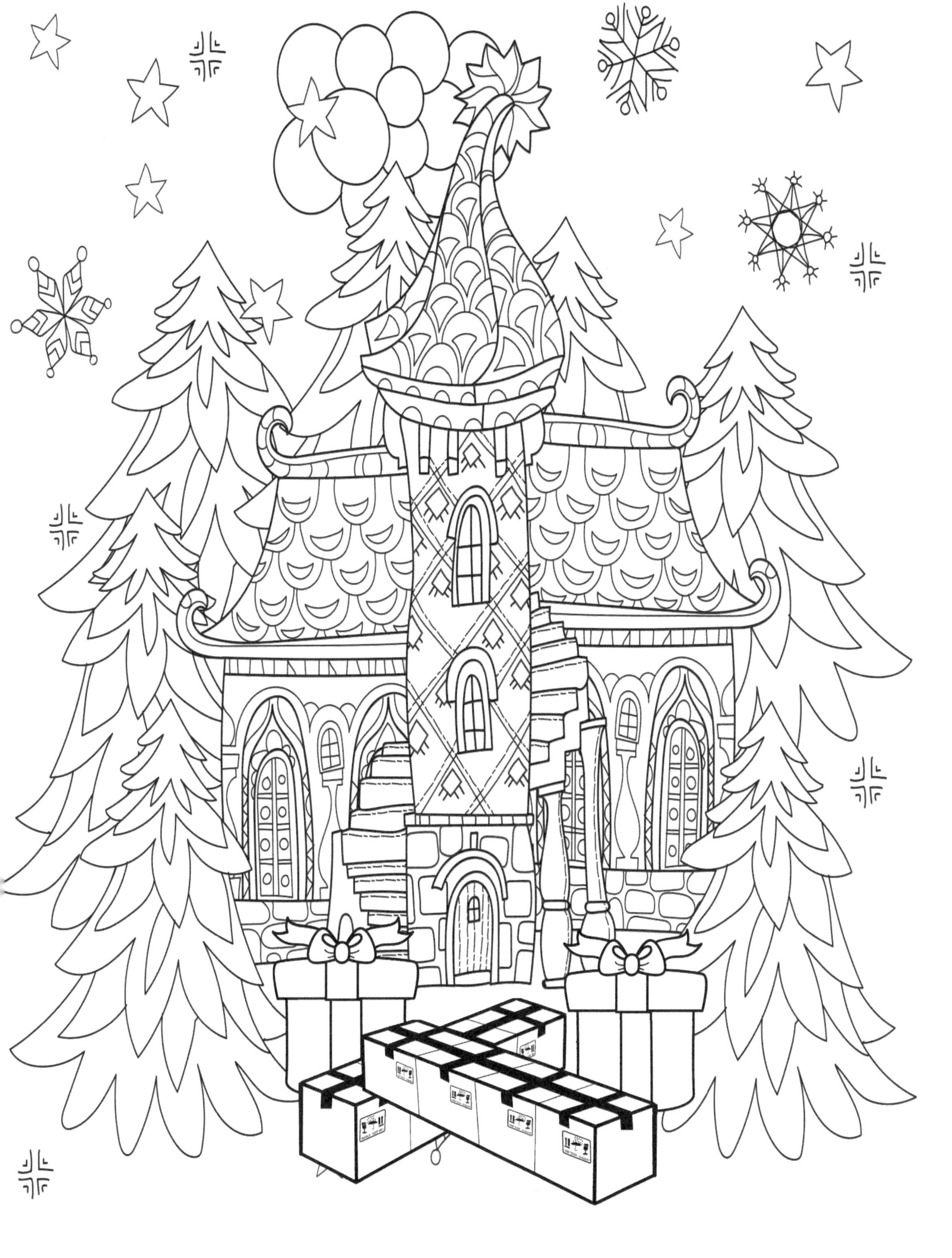

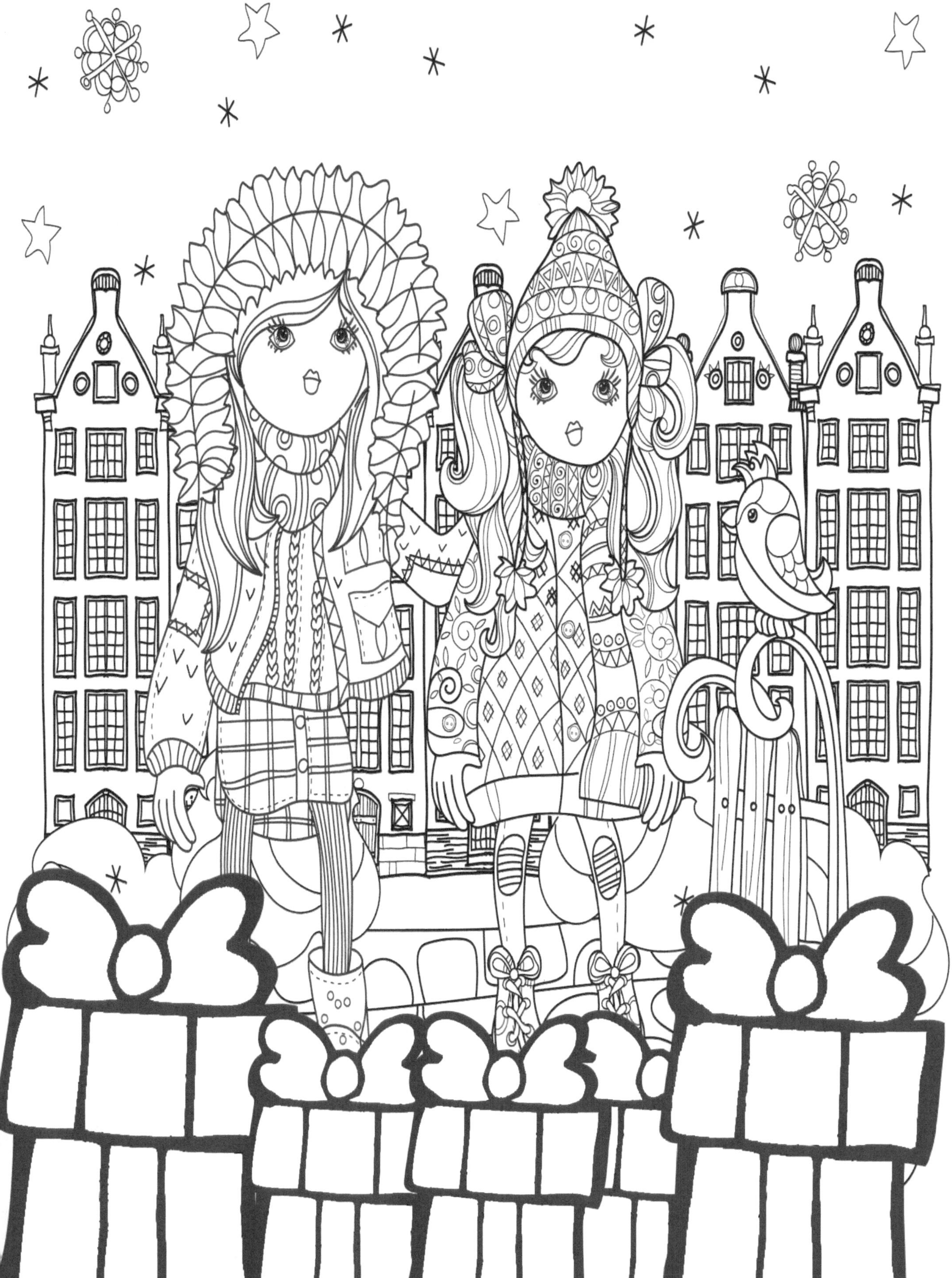

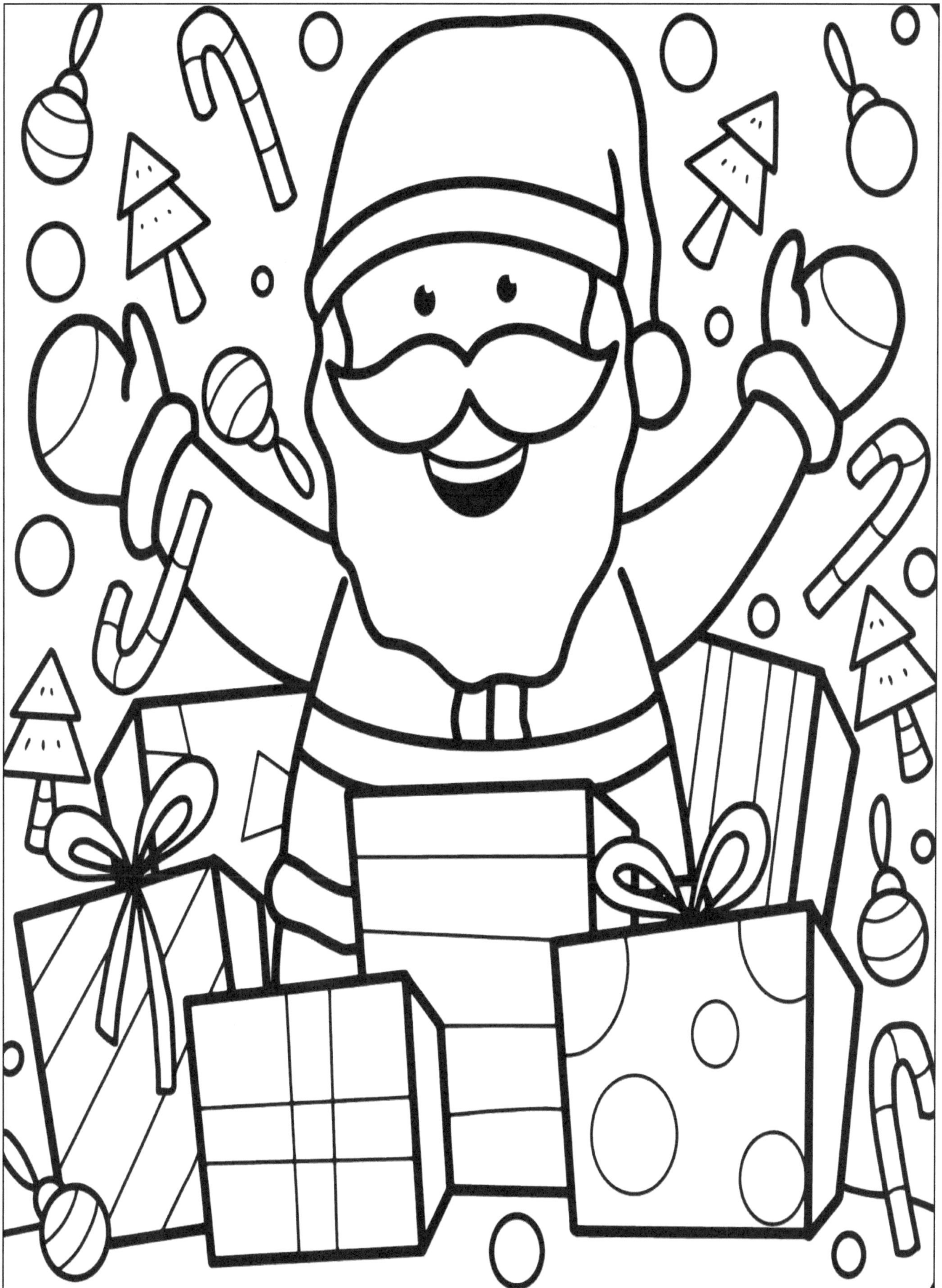

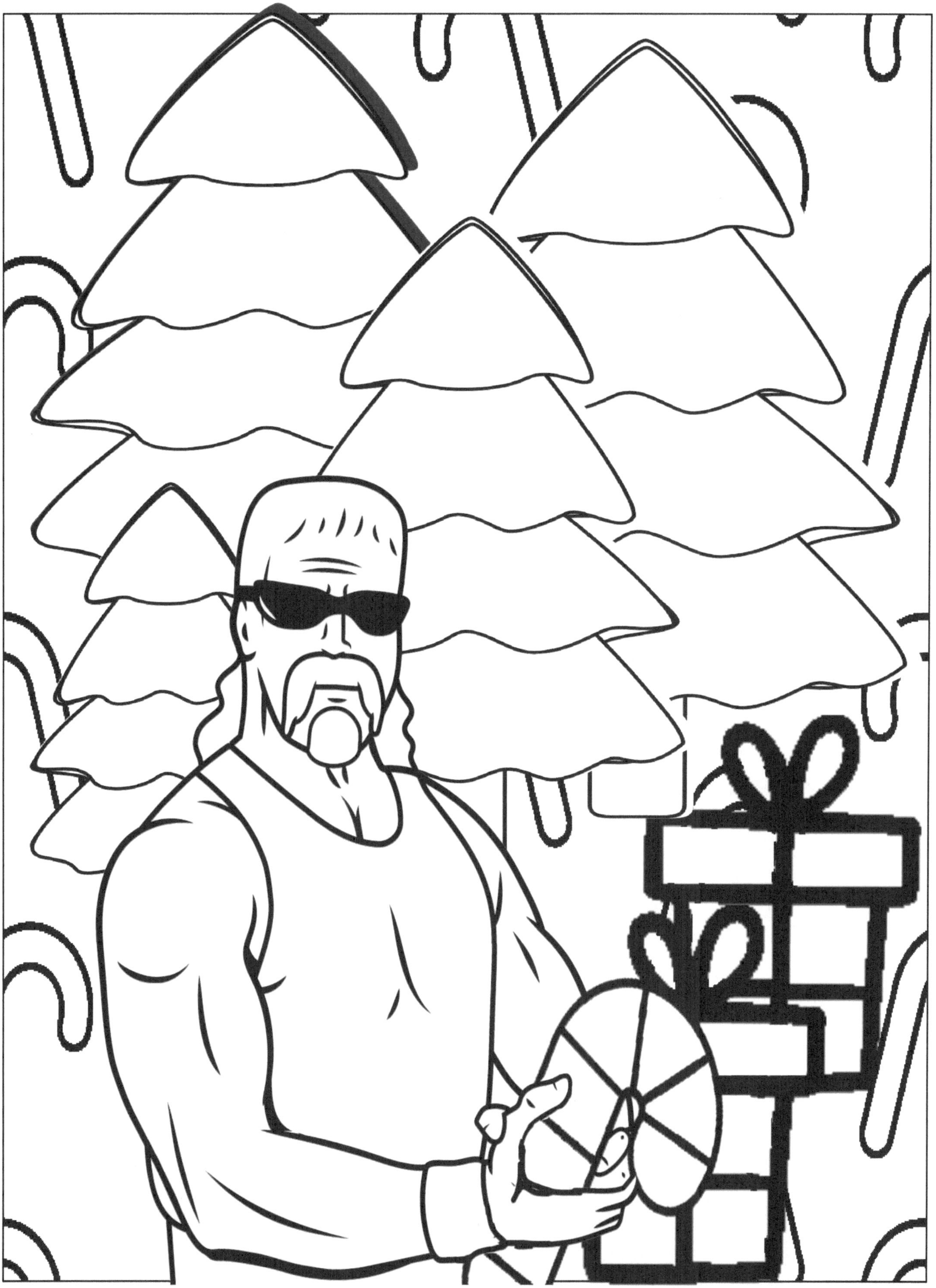

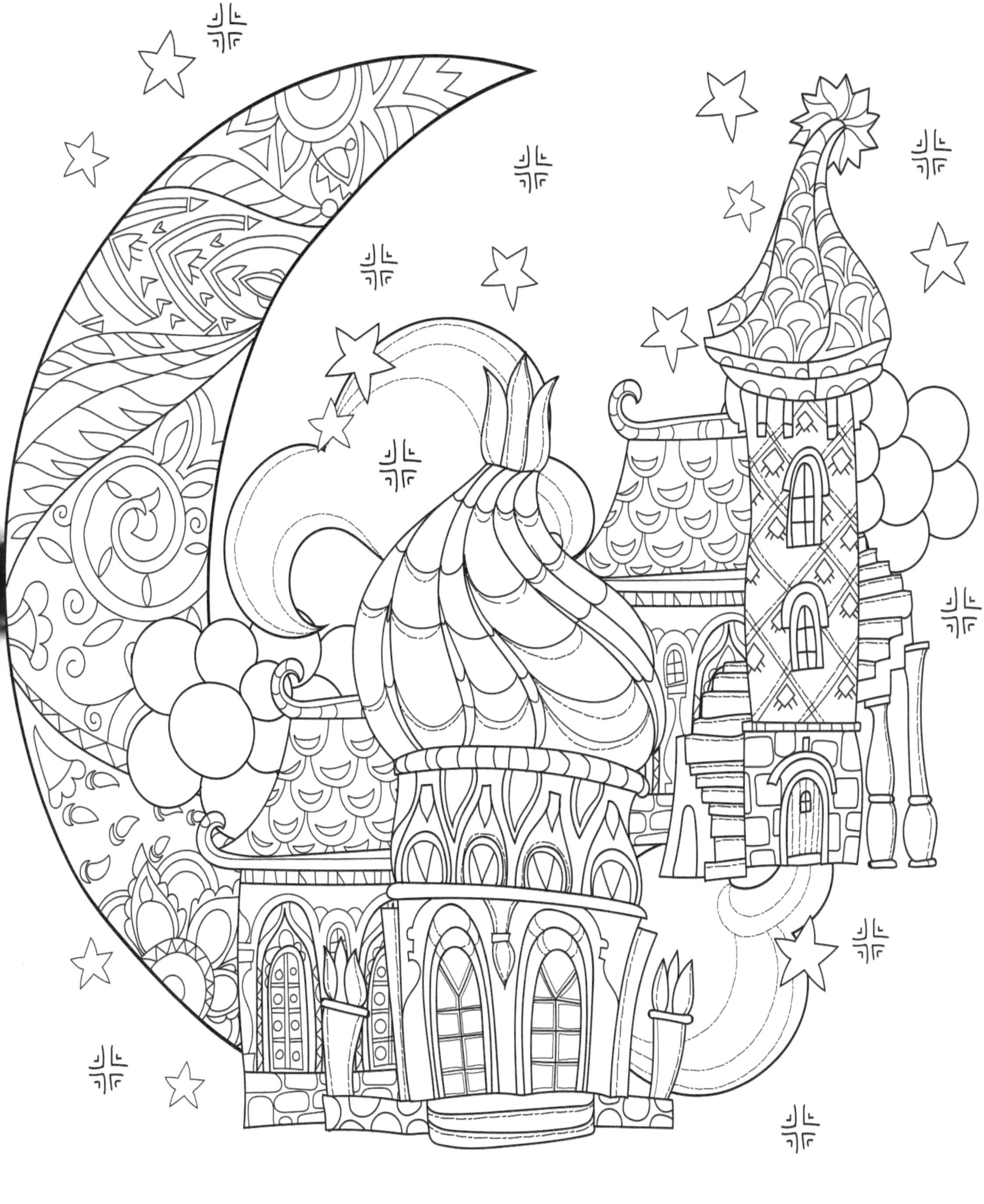

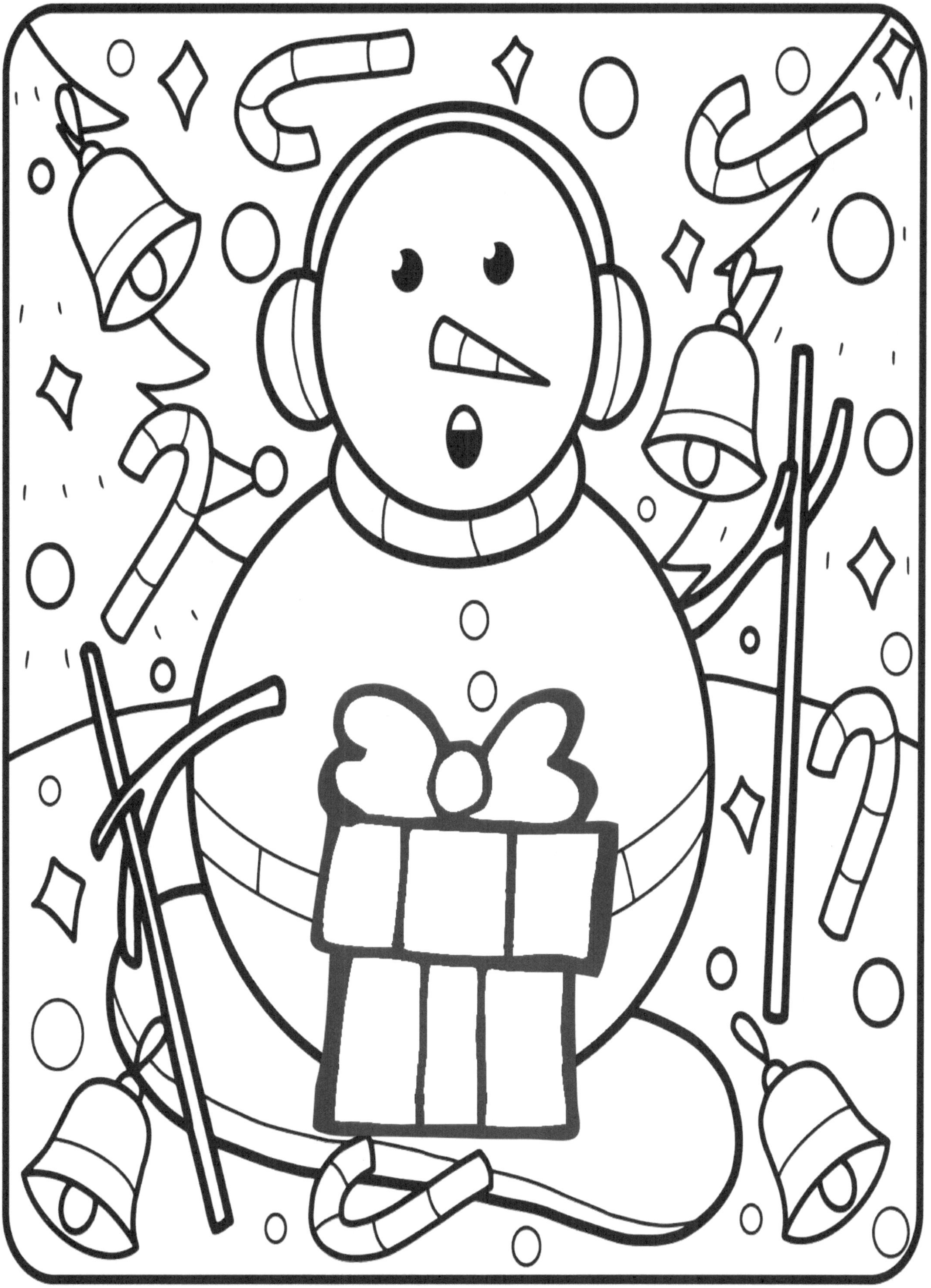

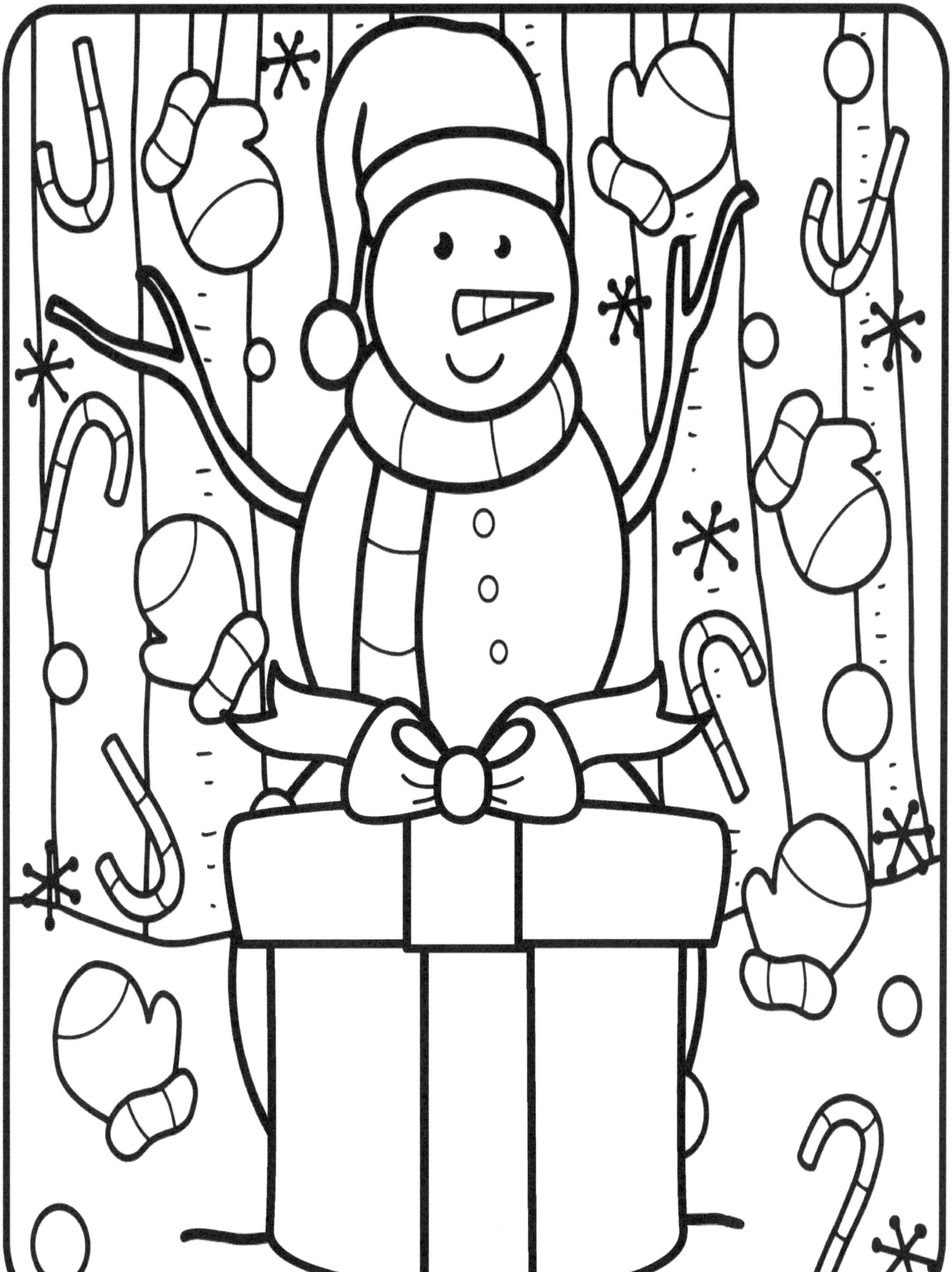

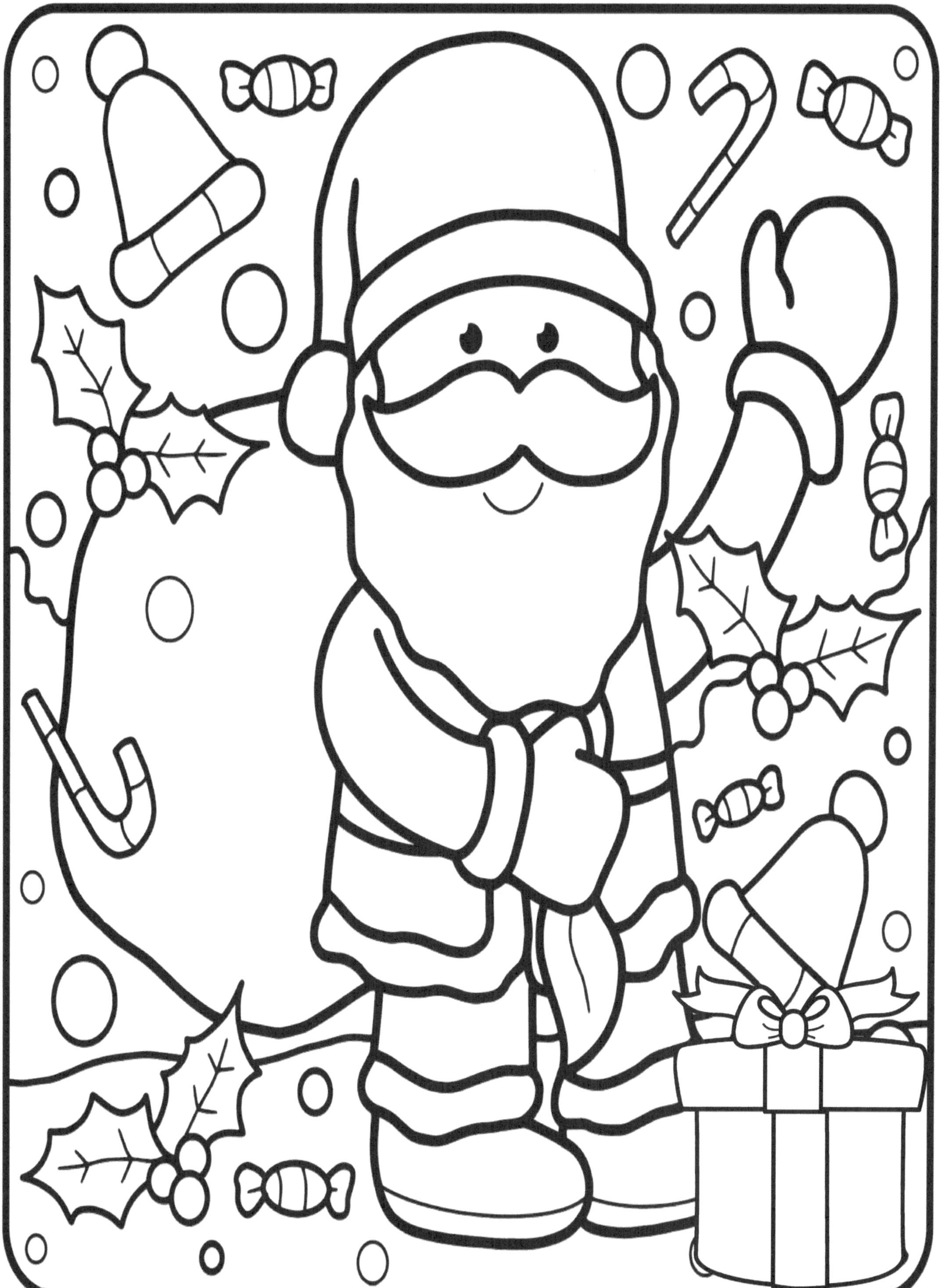

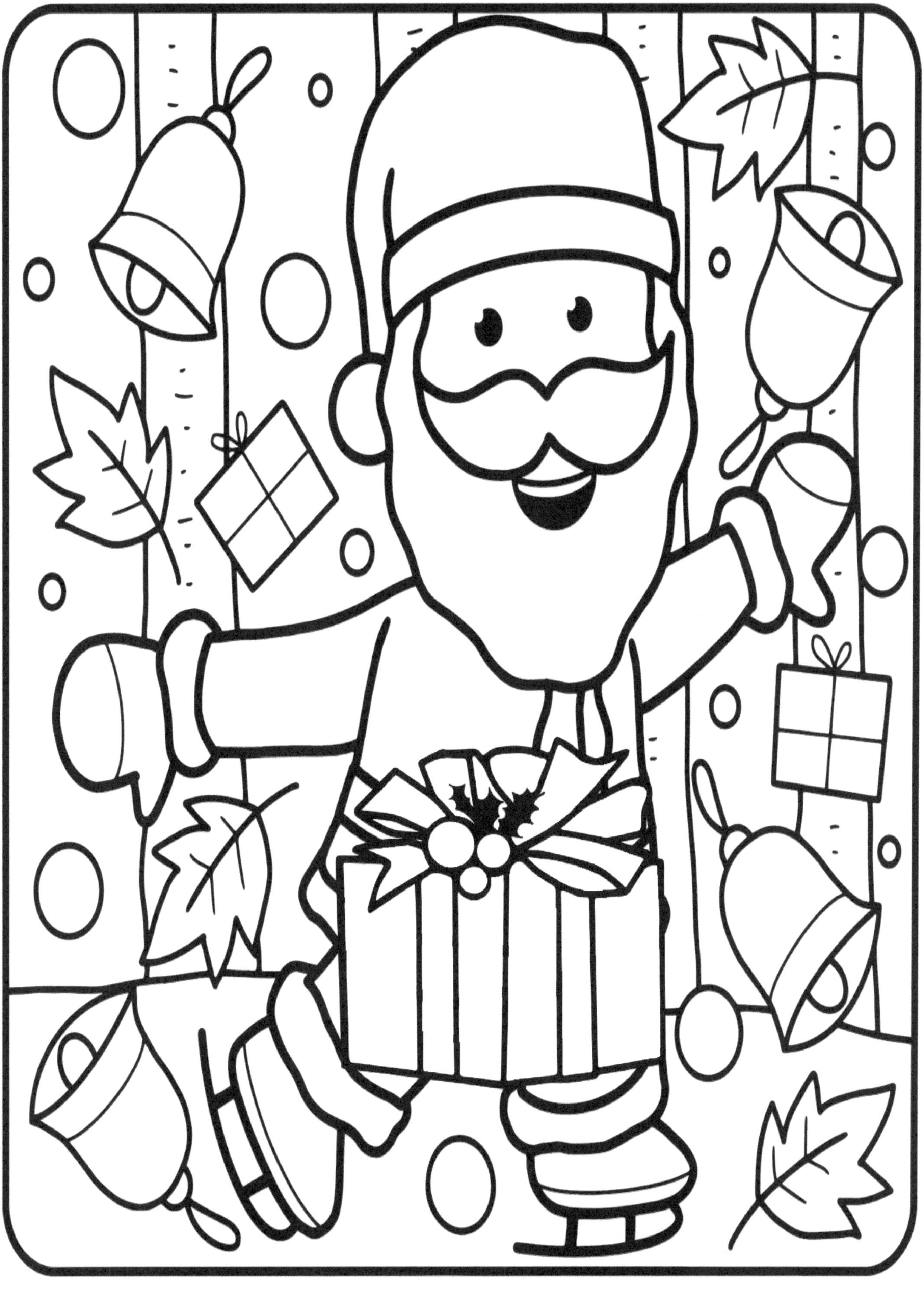

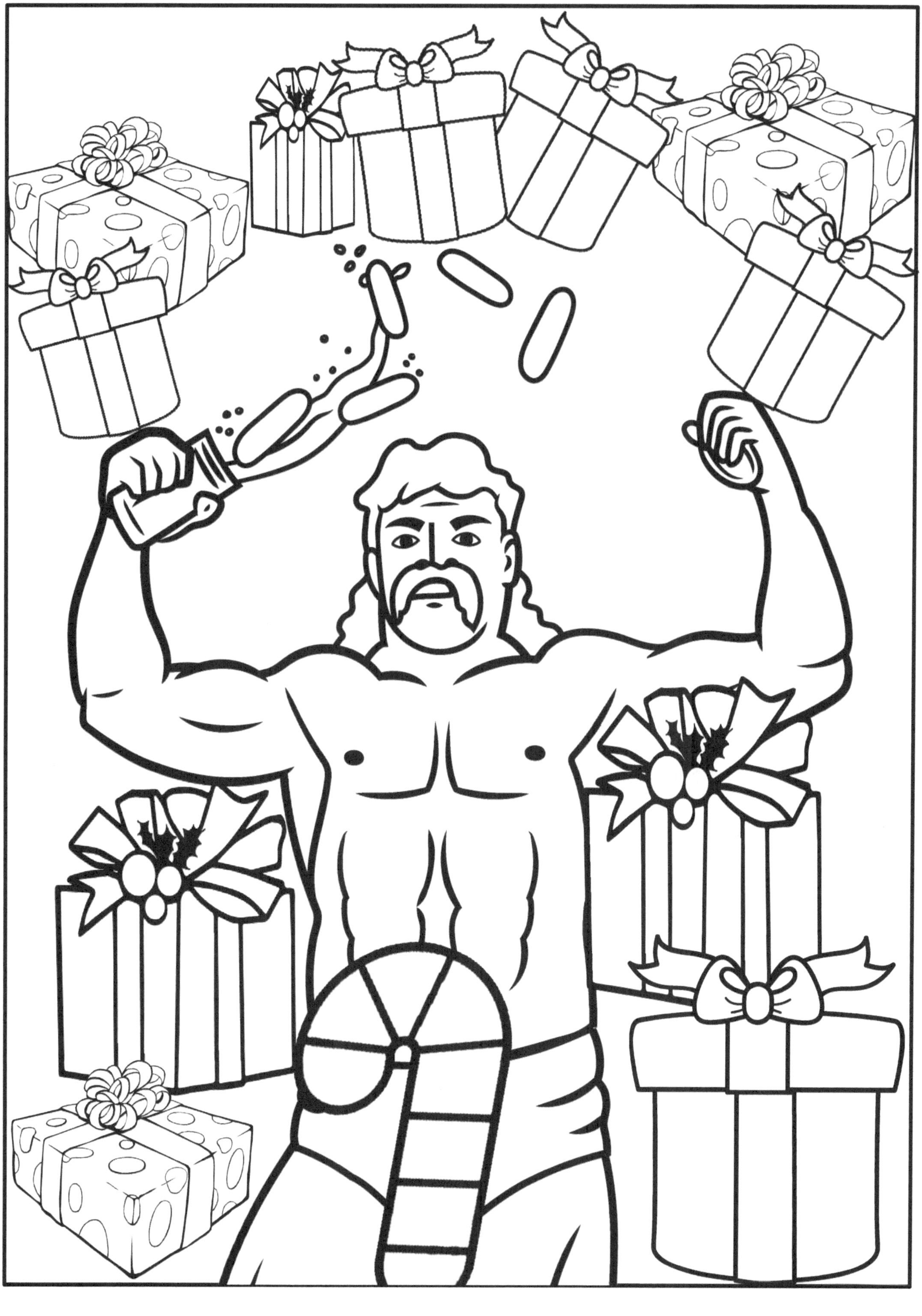

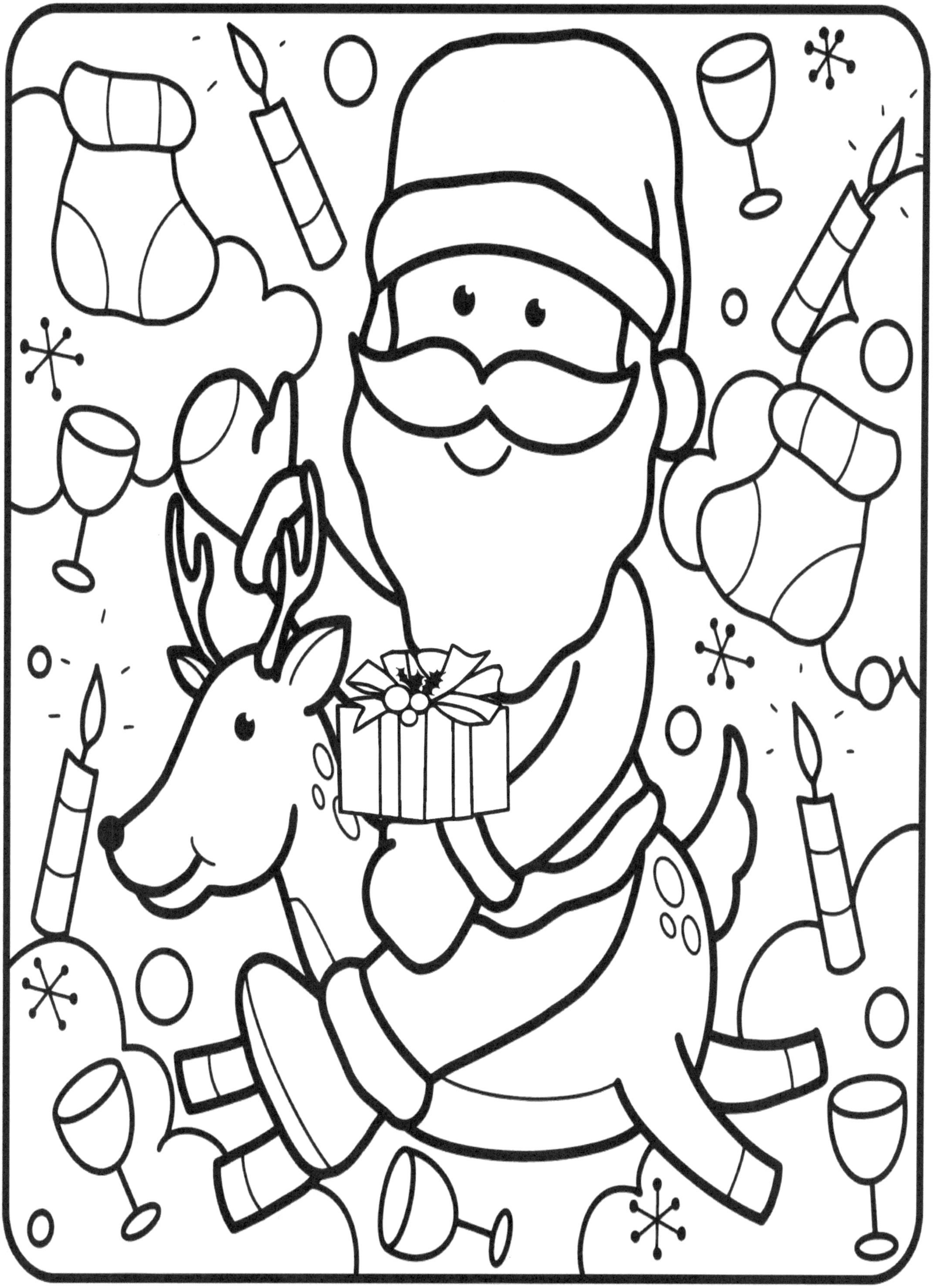

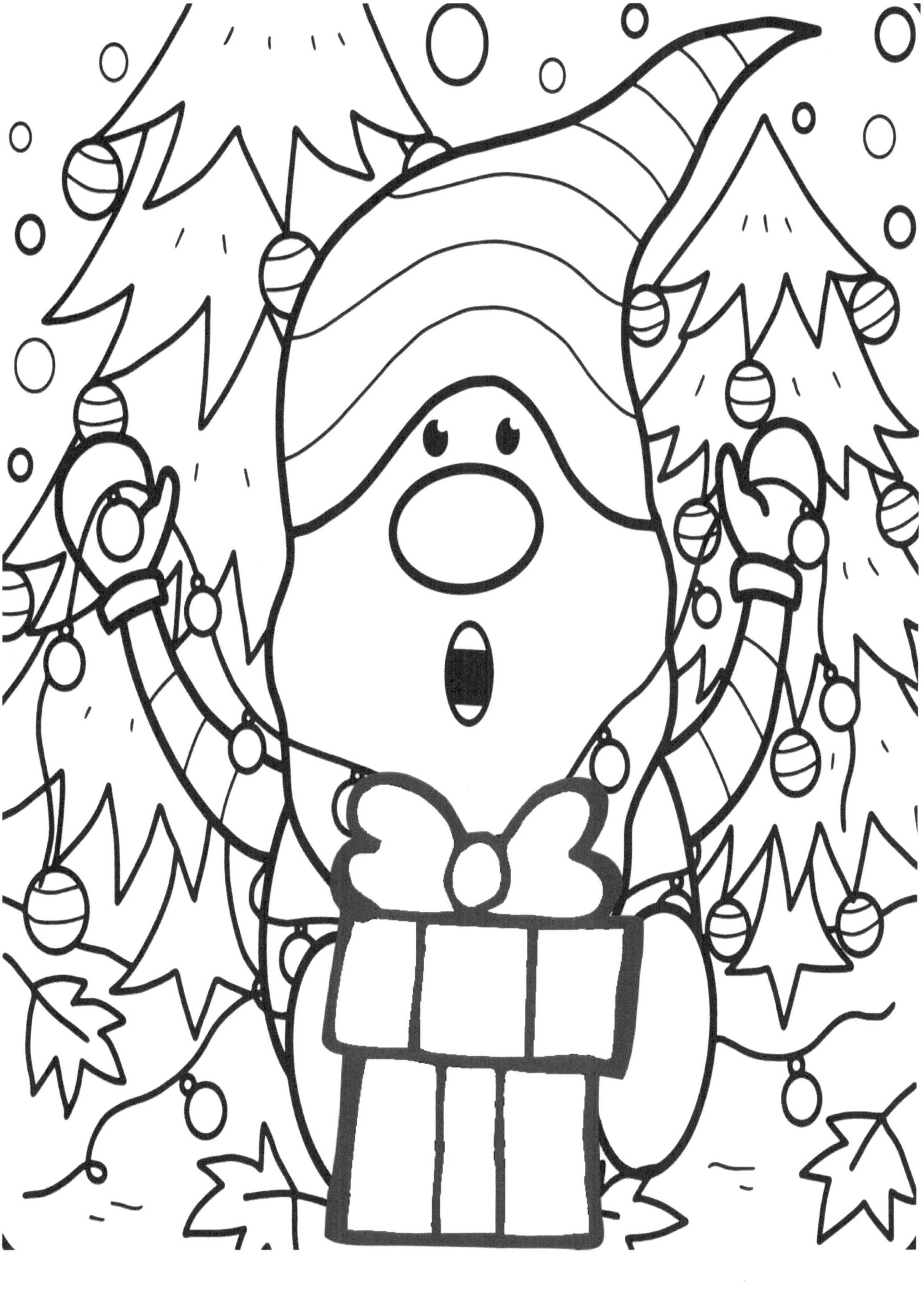

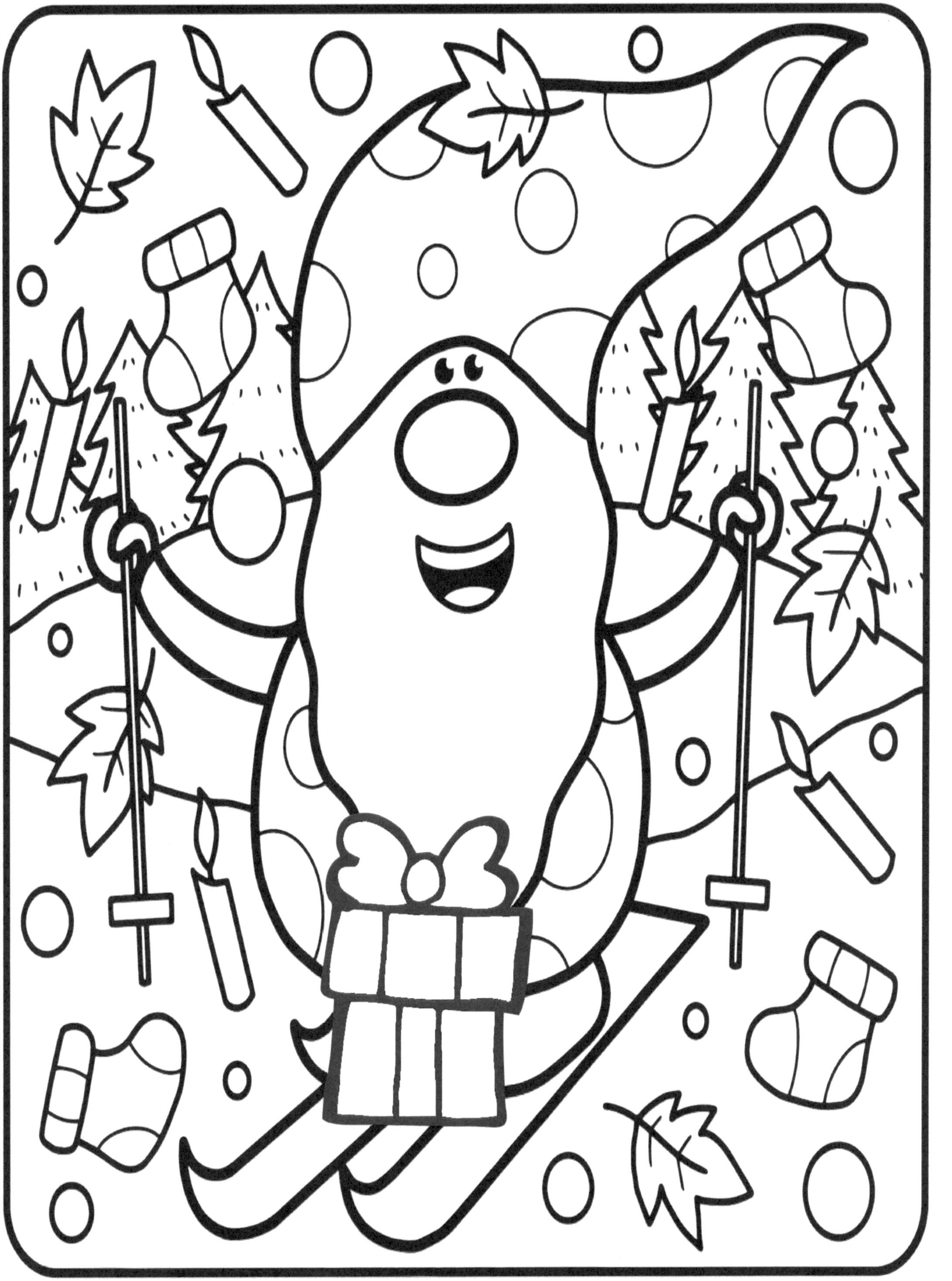

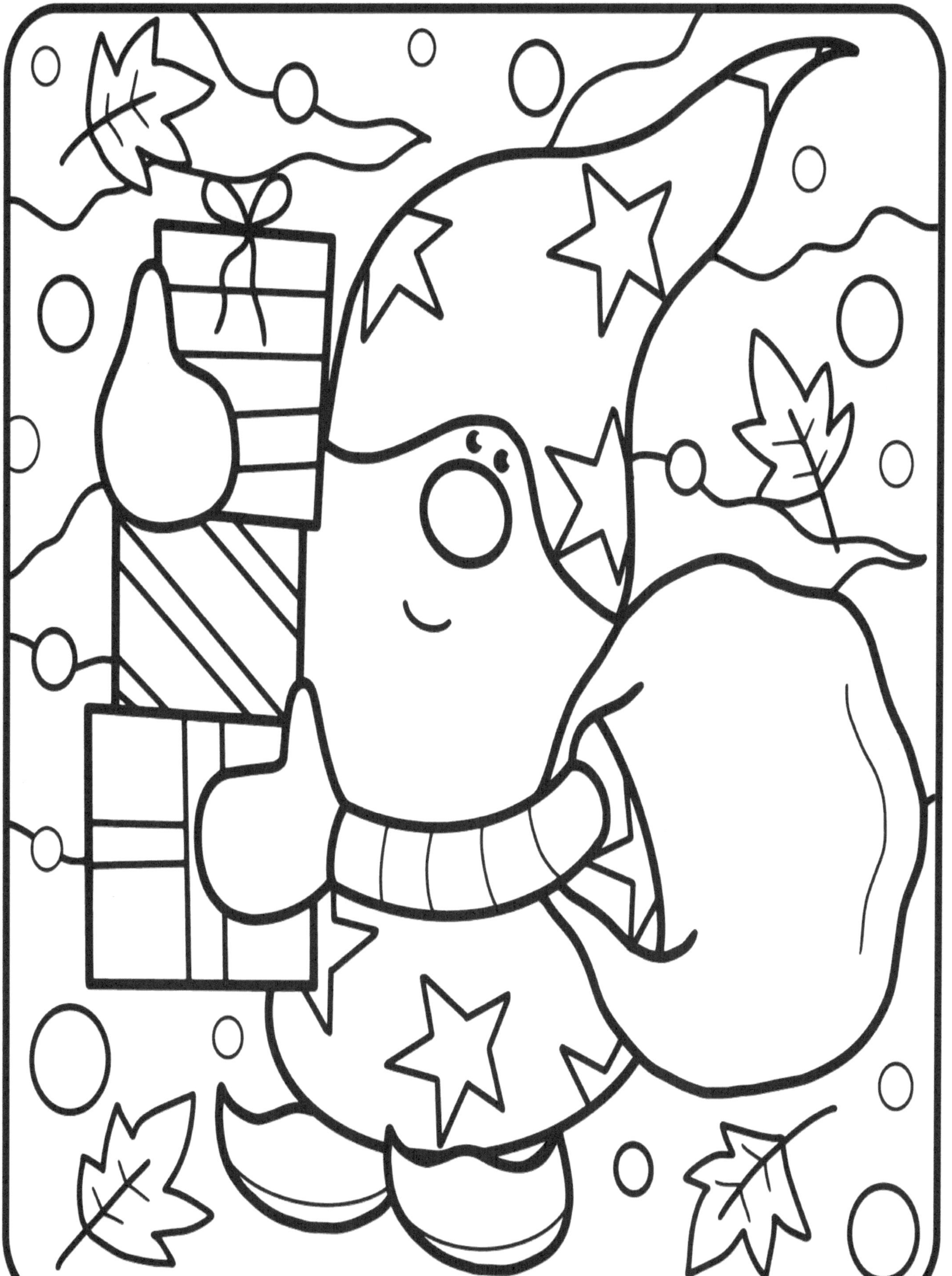

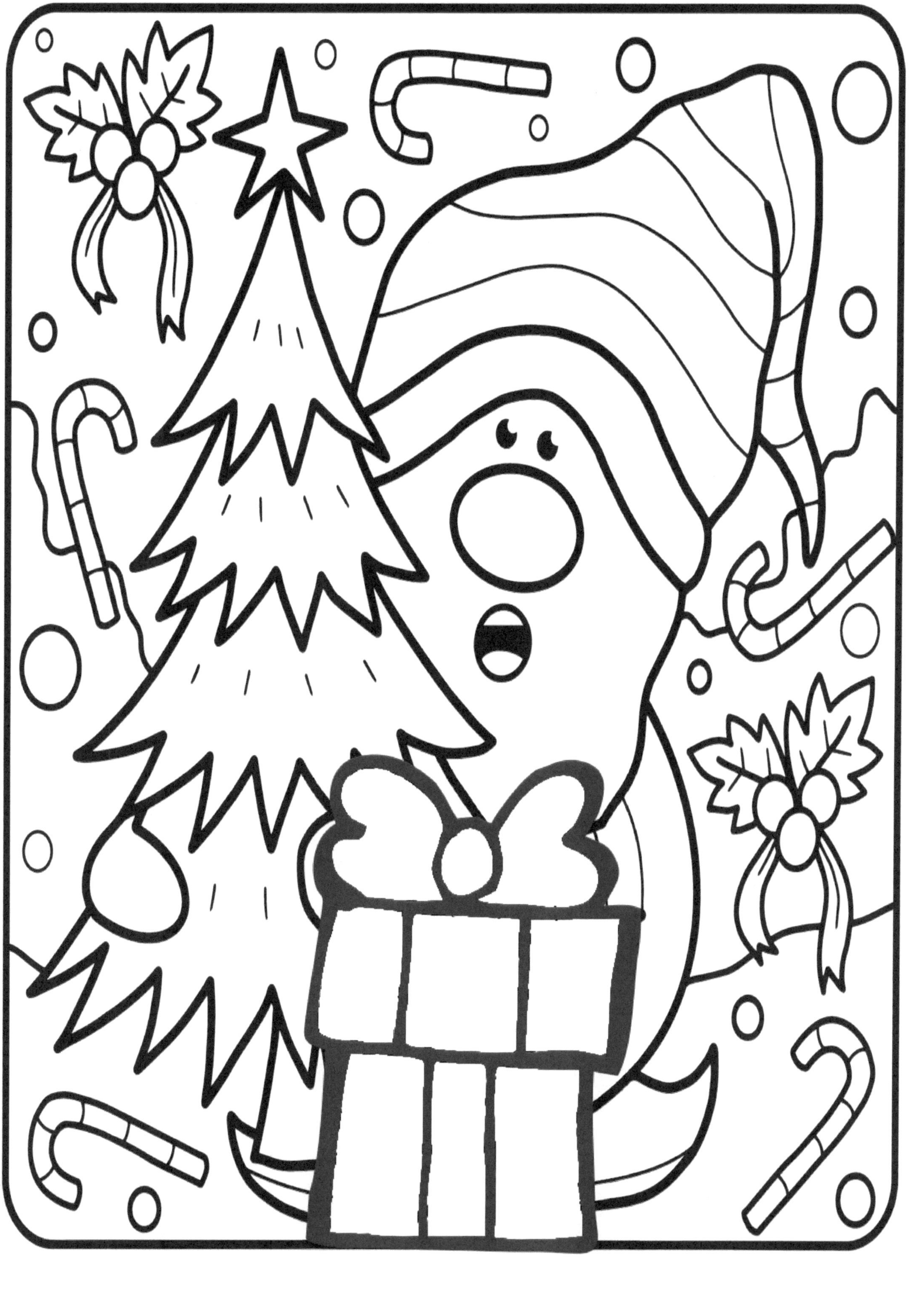

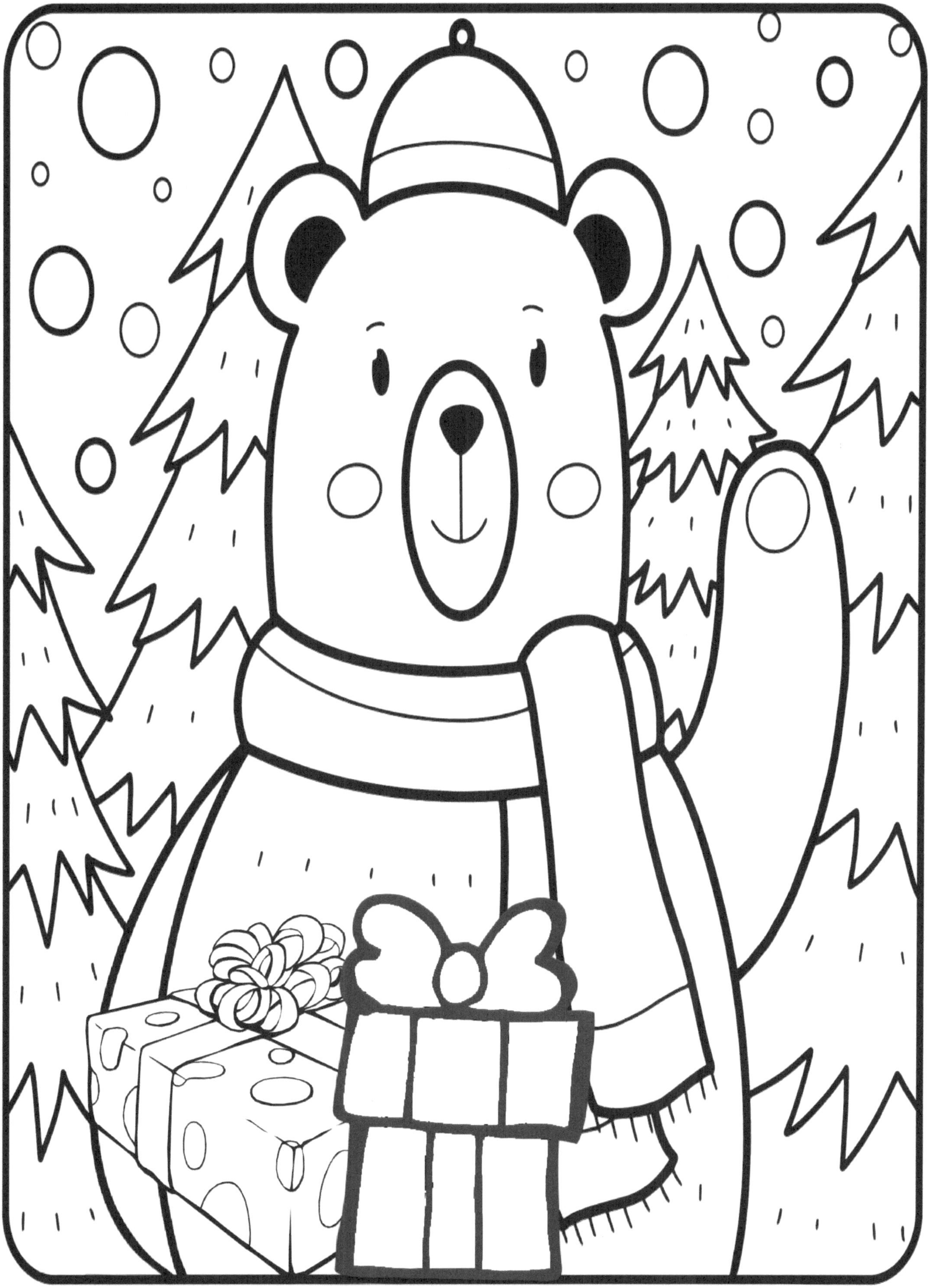

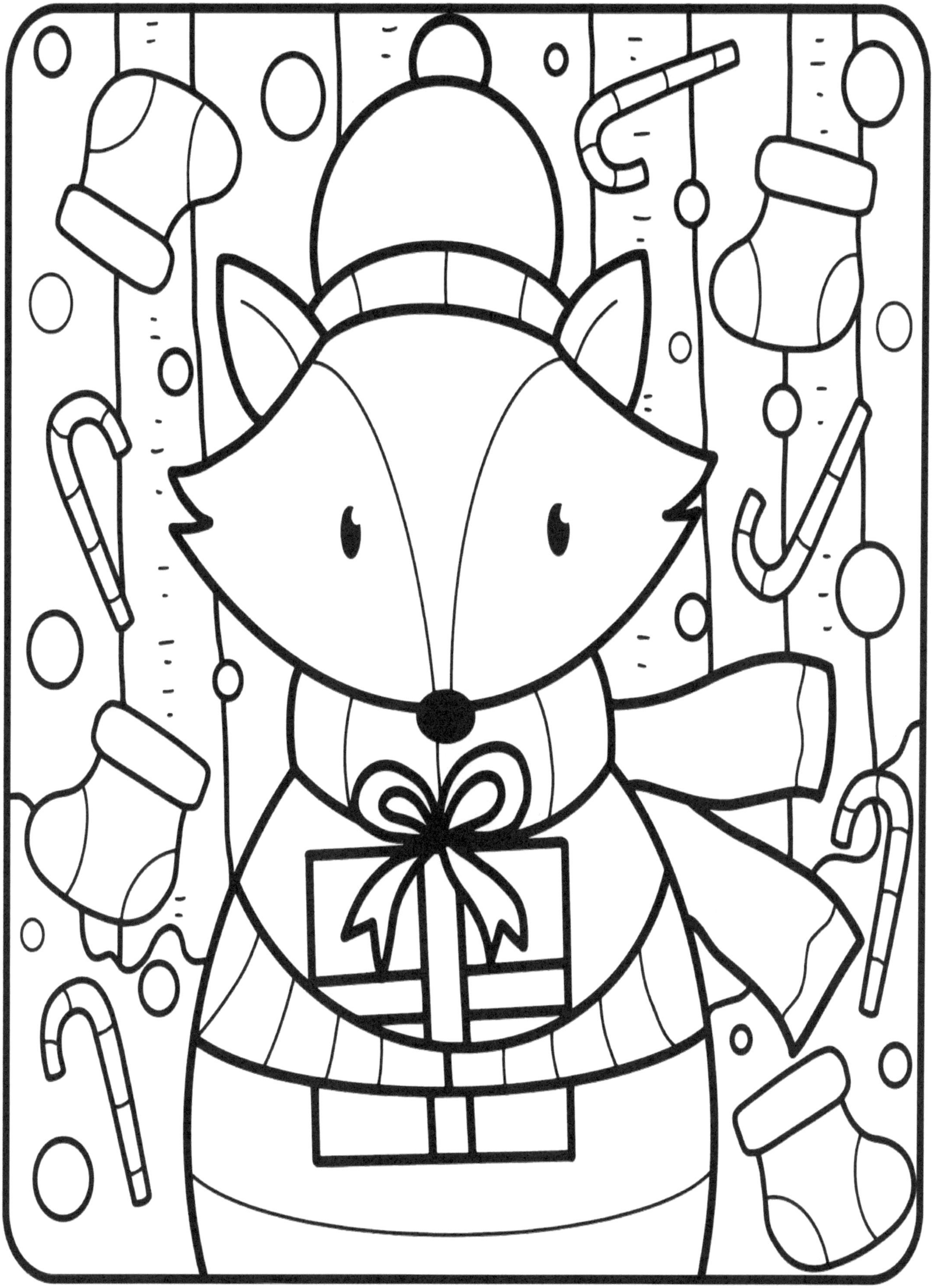

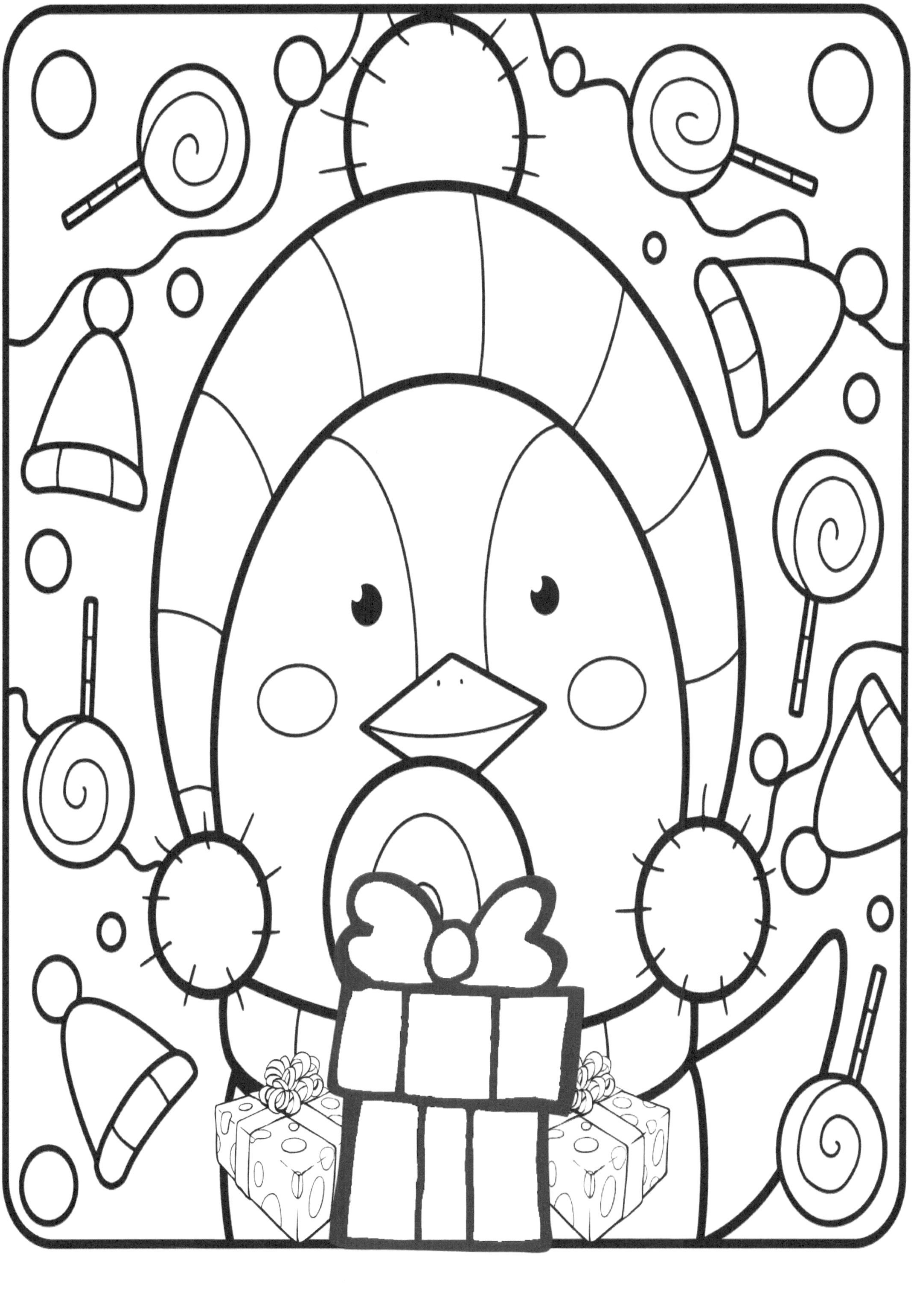

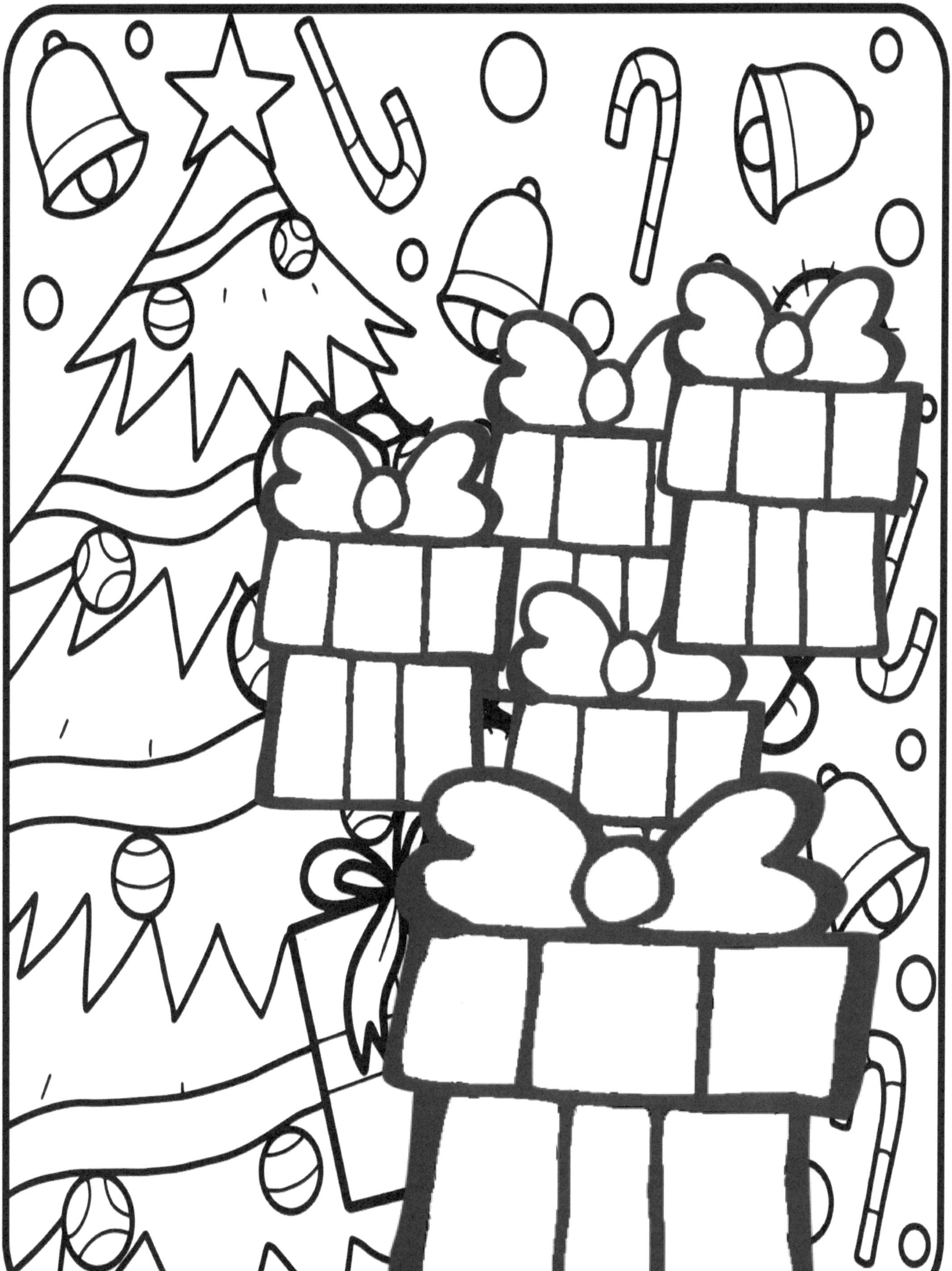

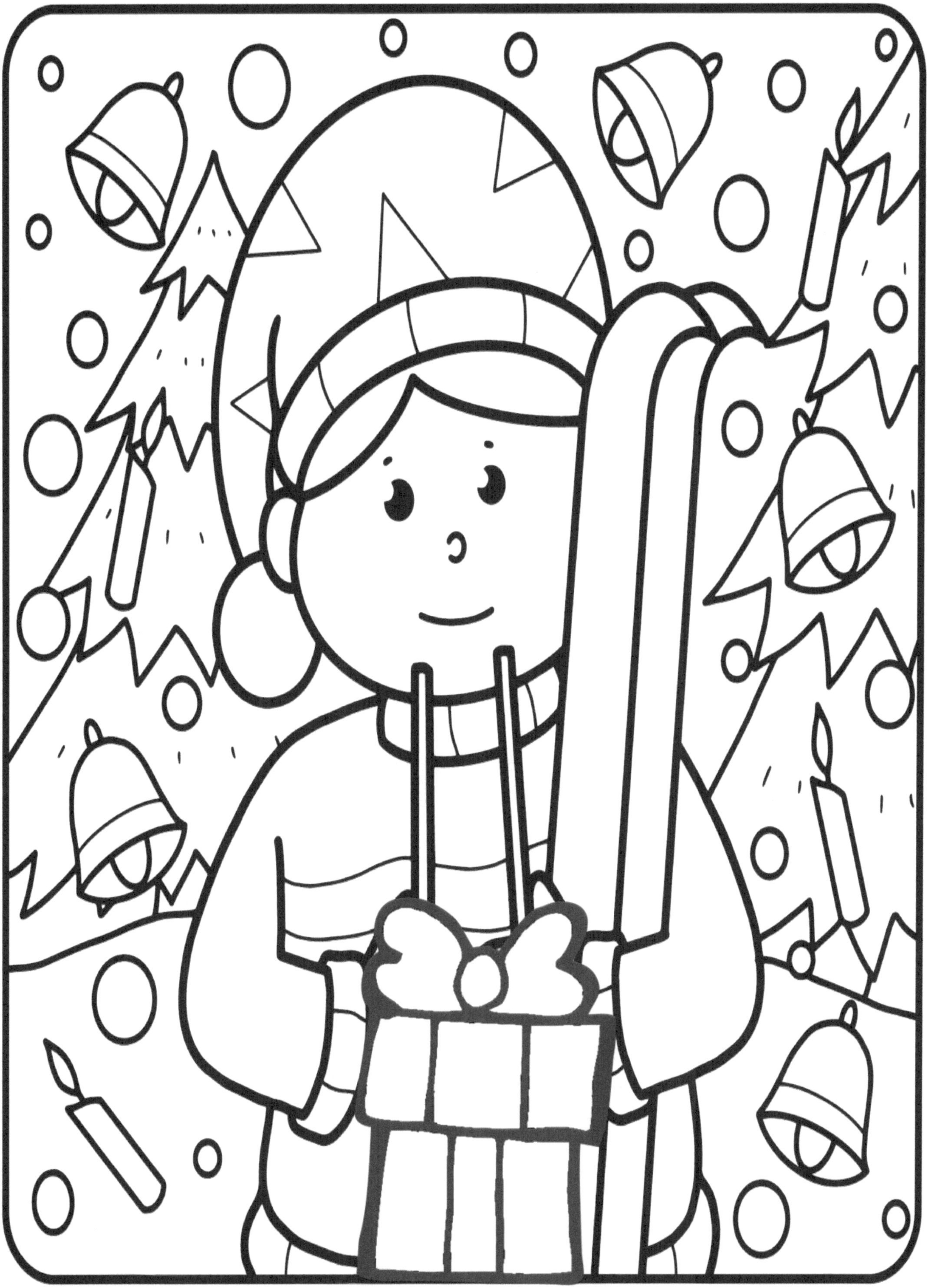

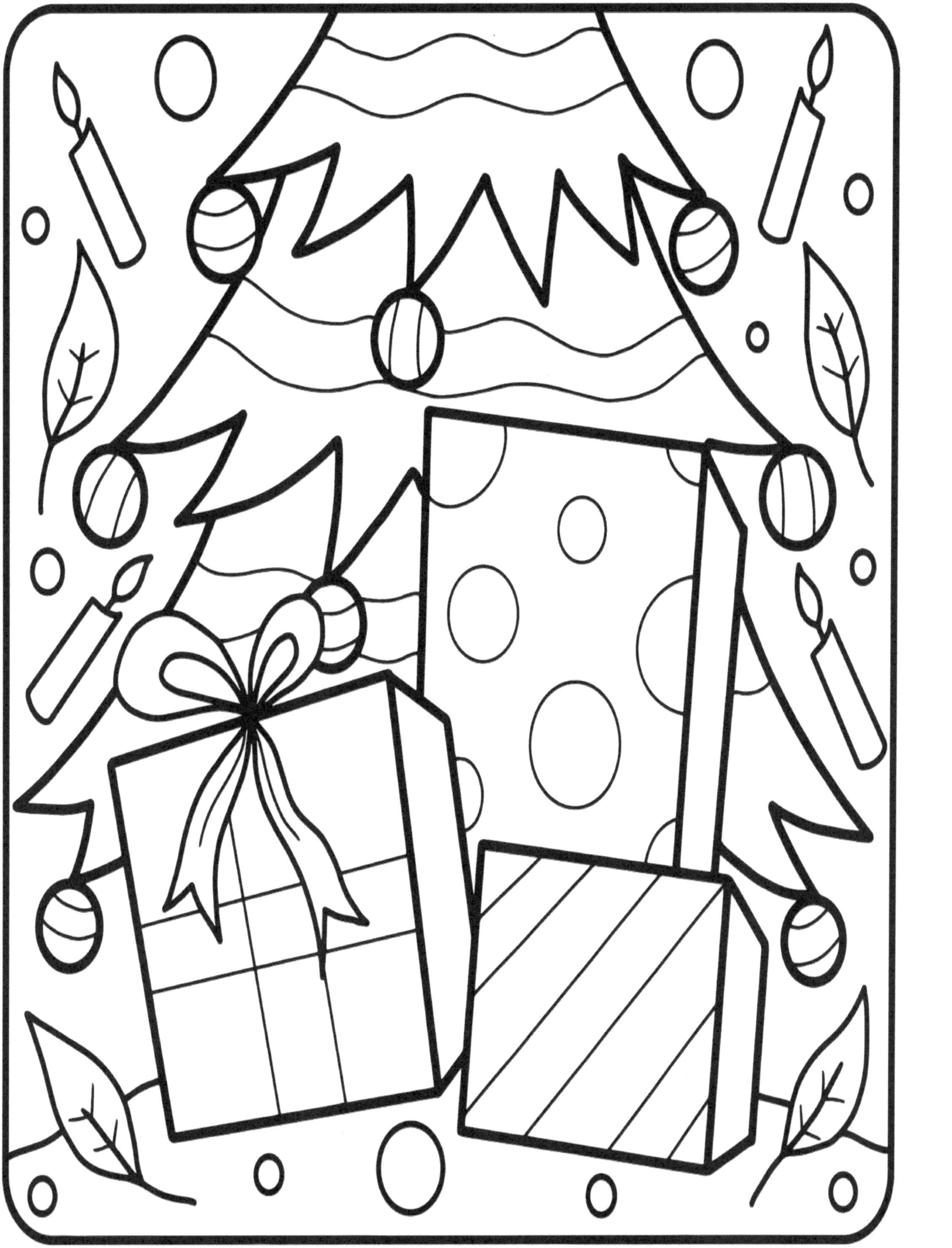

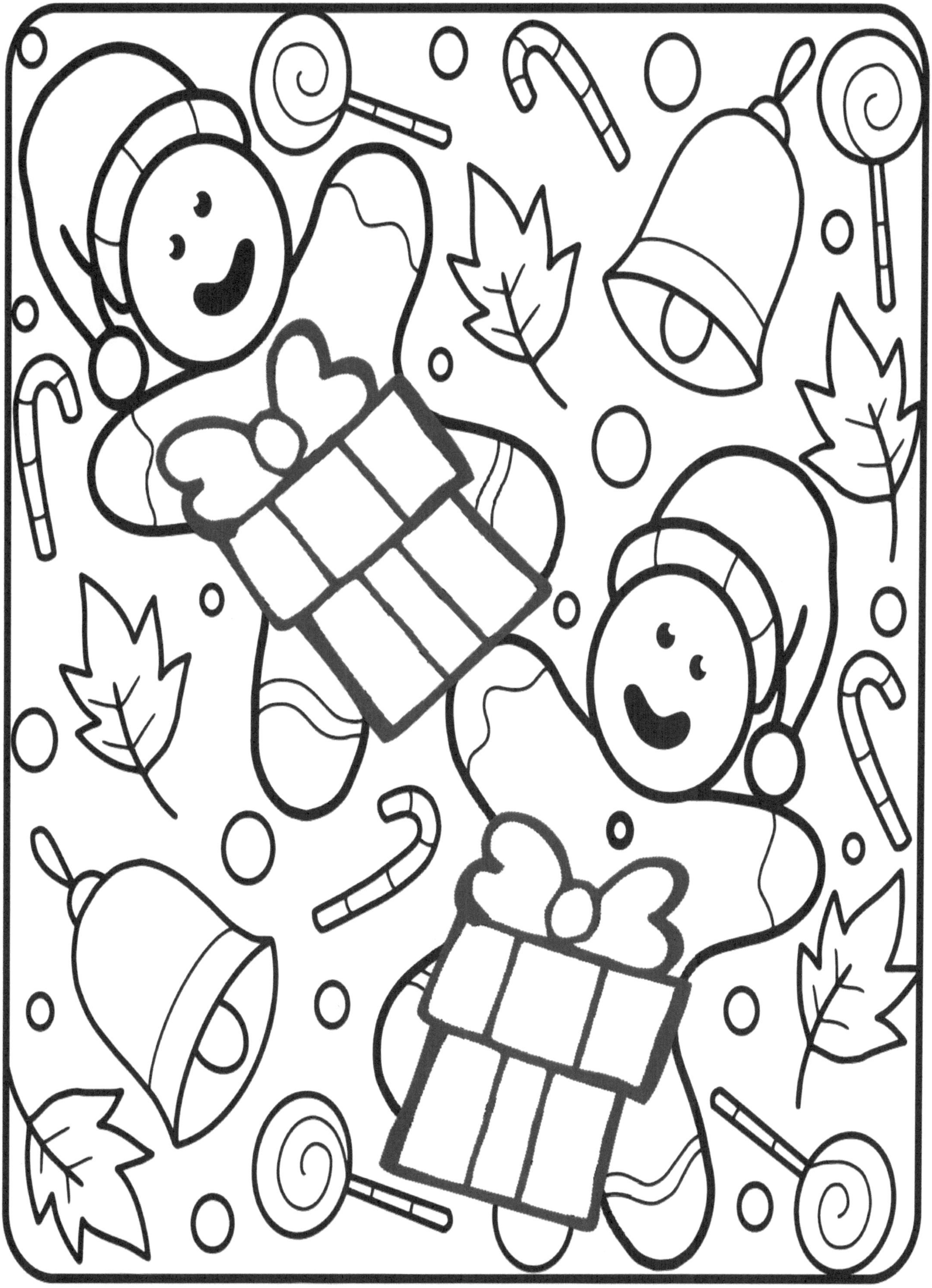

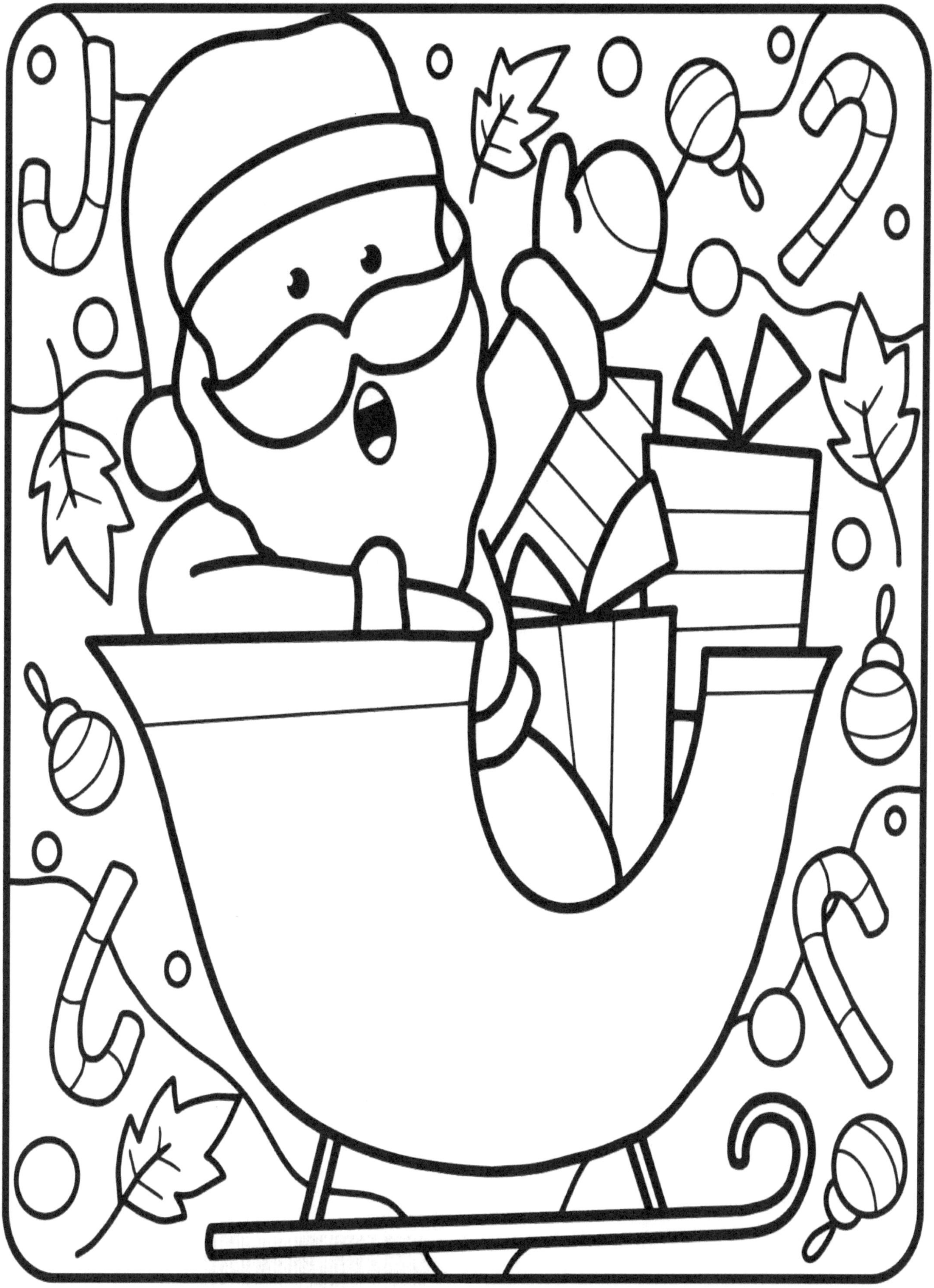

Made in United States
Troutdale, OR
10/04/2024

23425123R00060